Writ

Get Pa.

Repeat.

The Guide to Being a Successful Freelance Writer.

By Jyssica Schwartz

Published by

Cover Design by Christos Angelidakis

Edited by Amy Blocher

This book is dedicated to Geoff, whose support has never wavered, and is in honor of my parents, who have constantly cheered me on as I followed my dreams.

Table of Contents

FREE BONUS GIFT!

Just for downloading this book, I am offering you a **FREE** gift!

As a valued reader and a person with a story to tell, I'll send you a guide on **how to write a book in just three months**....and shhhh! A HUGE secret bonus, too!

To receive your present, click or go here: https://jyssicaschwartz. com/contact/free-gift-with-book/

To see what I'm up to or to just gaze in wonder at my majestic cat, you can follow me on Instagram, Twitter, or check out my blog on Medium.

Foreword by James Ranson

In the freelance writing world, you typically run into two kinds of people: **Writers** and **Hustlers**.

Writers are the creative types, always scribbling notes in a spiral notebook or swiping new ideas into an Evernote doc. Writers write because they love to do it, because it comes easily and naturally to them, because they're good at it, because they can't imagine doing anything else for a living. And for the most part, they turn out good-quality work that both they and their clients can be very proud of. Being a Writer is a noble, valuable, enjoyable calling that many intelligent, savvy people want to follow.

Unfortunately, many Writers have a major problem: they're broke.

See, Writers tend to know very little about business. They have little to no marketing experience, they don't know how to sell themselves or their services, and they are used to having their skills and talents be enough to bring them success. Many Writers find themselves playing the waiting game, hoping that a client will find them before they go into the red. Others manage to find work, but are so desperate for it that they accept insultingly low fees to work for clients who don't respect their talents. The fortunate ones can stick it out long enough to find a few good clients and build a referral base. But many throw in the towel and get a day job, clinging to writing as a beloved hobby where they once dreamed of being a full-time professional.

On the other hand, Hustlers are all about building and growing a business. Hustlers don't sit and wait for work to find them, they go out and look for it. They leverage connections, post all over social media, sign up for job search sites and writing gig forums, keep up a personal blog, learn marketing and sales techniques, and do whatever they can to bring in writing clients. Hustling is a badge of honor for entrepreneurs these days, and for the most part, the harder the Hustlers work, the more successful they perceive themselves to be.

Unfortunately, many Hustlers have *two* major problems: they're burned out, and they aren't producing quality work.

Hustlers aren't (usually) bad writers. They may in fact be very good ones. But hustling in the writing world usually means taking on as much work as humanly possible. A lot of the writing gigs out there (especially the easiest ones to find) are priced so low that to make a full-time living off of them, you either have to take on 80+ hours of them every week or you have to live in southeast Asia. The more work Hustlers take on, the less focus they have on doing any of it well and the less self-care they can keep up with to make sure their writing (and health) stays solid. Many Hustlers find themselves stuck in a never-ending grind, getting enough work to survive but not enough to get ahead. Others take drastic steps to reduce their overhead (such as actually moving to southeast Asia). The fortunate ones find gradually more lucrative gigs, or figure out systems to outsource a lot of the draft writing so that they can focus on ensuring the quality of the final result. But many throw in this towel as well, taking jobs that avoid writing entirely just so they can get out of what has become a full-on rat race.

You may be wondering: what does any of this have to do with the book you're about to read?

To put it simply, there's a third option, and the author of this book is it.

Jyssica Schwartz is a hybrid between Writer and Hustler. She combines the Writer's love for words with the Hustler's hunger for a healthy business, and puts them together into something that contains the strengths of both and the weaknesses of neither. In this book, Writers can learn from her marketing and sales experience without feeling overwhelmed or inauthentic. Hustlers can learn that it's possible to create a thriving writing business without sacrificing quality or sanity. And both can learn how getting paid well to write is honestly a lot easier than either of them thought it was.

How do I know this?

Because I used to be both. I started out as a Hustler, filling my hours and weeks with as many SEO articles and blog posts as I could get. And I burned out so hard on them within the first few months that I jumped on my pendulum and swung all the way over to being a Writer, waiting for the perfect clients to follow a star to me and fall down in worship. (Spoiler: it rarely worked.) Over a period of three years, I spent time in both camps, and neither one got my business where I wanted it to be.

When I first met Jyssica, I was in Writer space, and I honestly wanted her to shut up. She was so full of ideas and suggestions and advice about different marketing practices and sales strategies I could use in my business that it felt like she literally couldn't stop talking (even when I told her I wasn't interested, that I hated marketing, that I'd be fine doing things my own way, etc.). We eventually became friends, but I kept my distance from her professional advice, even as I saw her making money and finding clients more easily than I ever had. Then two major potential editing clients fell through in the same week, and I finally decided to eat some crow and start listening to her.

In a couple hours, we put together a basic sales strategy for my editing and ghostwriting business, and I started the first of four steps. Within two weeks, I had booked a five-figure client. In the following month, I had more referrals, discovery calls, interviews and prospects come across my desk than in the previous six months. (And I'm still mostly on the first step!) The best part is that I no longer feel like a Writer waiting or a Hustler grinding, but a…hmmm…a James James-ing. I feel like I'm doing what I should be doing and what I want to be doing, and that both the money and the quality are reflections of doing those things.

That's the power of Jyssica.

Now to be fair, I'll say that as you read this book, you may in fact also want Jyssica to shut up at first. She's about to throw a LOT of information at you, and you may want to run and hide in your Writer waiting room or your Hustler hub until it all goes away. If that's where you are, so be it. Just promise me (and yourself) one thing: that you won't stay there forever. Come back and give the hybrid life a chance sometime soon. You might struggle with it at first, but ultimately you won't regret it.

James Ranson
Wall Street Journal bestselling editor, ghostwriter and book coach
Atlanta, GA
james.m.ranson@gmail.com

Introduction:
Start Writing, Right Now

I met a stranger recently, and as we chatted he asked me what I do for a living. I told him, "I'm a writer and editor, and I do some sales consulting. What about you?"

He stumbled a bit and said, "I...I also write. But really, I am a <insert professional job title here>."

He stopped for a moment and explained he had never really heard anyone be so confident and casual about calling themselves a writer before.

I asked him, "Do you write? Regularly?"

"Yes, all the time, but..."

"Then you're a writer."

A writer is one who writes. Do you write with any regularity? Do you blog, or journal, or write political rants? Do you do writing prompts on Reddit or jot down story ideas on scraps of paper that are currently occupying your nightstand drawer, maybe taking up space on your refrigerator, or a small notebook somewhere?

I happen to be a paid and published writer. You may be aspiring to be paid, but you're already a writer.

Do you want to be a writer, but are not one yet?

Start writing. Right now. Put down the book and go sit in front of your computer or with your laptop on your lap on a comfy couch or hold a spiral notebook, and put down some words. Use the phrase "I am a writer." Say it out loud, and then write down anything which comes to mind.

It doesn't matter if your words are terrible on this try, or if they're silly or funny, or super serious. It doesn't matter if they don't tell the story you've always envisioned.

What matters is just getting those first words out of you and onto the page. Getting started is the hardest step, as taking that first step of any journey always is, but once you start the floodgates will open.

Just remember, it is easier to delete or change existing writing than it is to start from scratch on a blank page. That stark white page just sits there, sterile and taunting, leeching the ideas right out of your head.

When people ask me how I got to be a writer, or what they can do to become one, I always answer: Just write. Right now, pick up a pen and write a list, or what you want for dinner, or a paragraph about the vacation you took last year. Writing anything is better than having nothing on the page, and once you have words down, your mind will wander; you'll find inspiration.

As you write, you'll keep writing, and then more will come, and you may find yourself with a blog, or a YouTube channel, or writing comic strips which make you laugh, or as a contributing writer on a website, or maybe writing a book!

You will find that the more you write, the more you have to say.

If you want to be a writer, there is only one requirement, **write**. If you want to be PAID to be a writer, there are other steps. But it starts with that first word.

Now, let's make some money with that writing.

Chapter 1:
I Am a Writer

I have been a writer since before I knew what that meant. I made up my own lyrics and songs as a kid, I wrote stories about my imaginary twin sister and my pets, and kept a journal starting when I was about 4 years old. I still have those journals. There is a shelf in my house dedicated to the 12 or so journals I've dragged along since childhood.

Writing is both a creative outlet and a necessity to me.

I have lists of tasks, things to do, groceries to buy, reminders, etc. I learn and understand things best and will remember it better if I write down. In high school and college, I had poor study habits, because I would take very diligent handwritten notes in class. Once I write it down I just remember it, so I didn't need to learn the best ways to study. Eventually, though, learning good study habits made learning easier and I was able to learn even more effectively!

I write down dates, so I remember birthdays, doctor appointments, and the number of every credit card I've ever had. I know phone numbers and never use my contact list to call family members or close friends.

I write for fun, making up silly stories, writing and doodling a ridiculous comic to make my husband laugh, or making up on-the-spot parodies of songs in the shower, like I'm the next Weird Al, and singing with gusto. I write music. Not just parodies, but melodies and lyrics, beautiful songs that make me happy to have created them, and even happier to sing them.

I have notes all over the place with ideas for books, stories, songs, poems, and other things.

I write for myself, like with my blog. My ridiculous, random, variety-filled blog which makes me smile. Everything from rants, fun facts, political essays, comics, to recipes, how-to articles, advice, and other fun stuff. It entertains me and is an outlet for my creativity.

I write for publications. I have contributed articles to *Huffington Post, Lifehack, Thrive Global,* and more. I write professional articles and put them on LinkedIn and Medium to grow my network and build a community. I write for exposure, and because I want to entertain, educate, and make people think or make them smile.

I write and edit for clients. I do blogging, website copywriting, ghostwriting, ad copy, email templates, documentation, and even branched out into book editing.

I write.

That's it. I am a writer. I am a weirdo, a cat lover, an adopter of penguins, an optimist, a wife, a sister, a daughter, and a writer.

In 2016, I finally took the leap of seeing if people wanted to pay for my words. Awesomely enough, it turned out that some people did. I am now a paid writer of all diverse kinds things. Website landing pages, ad copy, blog posts, ghostwriting books, press releases, email templates, sales scripts, and anything else a client needs. I even do some sales consulting, as that has been my specialty for so many years.

Finding out people would pay me was probably the most exciting and terrifying thing I have ever done in my life, and I've been skydiving. I had to research and learn on the fly about contracts, invoicing and pricing (lots of research on this one!), 1099s, what to do about taxes, how to incorporate, and everything a business requires. It was extremely stressful and scary, but at the same time, it was also satisfying in the way I genuinely hoped it would be.

The reason I didn't take this risk years before was because of a fear of it not being what I wished for. You know that feeling. You SHOULD like something; it SHOULD fulfill you, like you're supposed to be happy because it is a well-known thing that people are happy doing?

That was my biggest fear, and what really kept me from trying to become a paid writer sooner. What if I had done all this work to become a writer, and either failed spectacularly at it…**or succeeded, but wasn't happy?**

Fear of failure wasn't quite enough to stop me, but the idea that the one thing I have always wanted to do, besides become an astronaut, might not be fulfilling, was almost enough to scare me off.

Being an entrepreneur is a major goal for a lot of people, and the millennial generation is more entrepreneurial than previous generations – by a lot.

According to the 2016 BNP Paribas Global Entrepreneur Report, the millennial generation are starting businesses earlier than the baby boomers did, and they are starting so many more of them, plus they are putting more emphasis on being socially conscious.

I had not been dreaming of being an entrepreneur and building a business, to be honest. I actually was perfectly happy working for my last boss, as he was my boss for several years and became a close friend. He is still my friend, and he always encouraged me and supported my training and growth, and I am incredibly lucky he also encouraged me in my path to being a writer, even when it meant leaving my job to pursue it.

Sometimes I still think that if someone wanted to hire me full-time to be a writer and editor, I would say sure! Why not? YOU take care of the taxes and retirement account, the benefits, and take on the liability!

But being an entrepreneur has been thrust upon me so that I can live my dream, and I am absolutely in love with it. Sure, taxes are more annoying now and I'll certainly never get a refund again! Yes, it's a bit more paperwork, and the responsibility is all mine. The sales and business development are all on me. No backup plans or safety nets.

On the other hand, I am very Type-A, very organized, and I am loving every second of being my own boss. I am in the exact right moment in my life, the stars are perfectly aligned to allow me to do this.

In the few months before starting my own business, I turned 30, quit smoking, and went low-carb, which made me lose almost 20 pounds. I was doing really well at work and had just gotten a big raise! Honestly, everything was coming up roses. I was happier and healthier than I'd ever been, and as a middle-class-raised kid, I was making more money than I ever thought I would. I was married to my best friend. For the first time in my adult life, I really felt I was on the right path in every area of my life.

My work didn't fulfill me on a soul-deep level, but I was good at it and it was lucrative. But changing and growing, and becoming happier on a personal level opened my eyes to other possibilities and gave me the courage to try to find my passion.

Besides, in the absolute worst-case scenario, I fail at being a writer and go back to a business development job in an office. You know, that thing I have a decade of experience in and a great track record. It's not like trying to start my own business was going to cancel out my previous career or the opportunities it held for me.

So, it was either try and fail and still have a good life, or try and not fail and be a writer.

On my journey, I have met some amazing people, worked for great clients who have opened my eyes to innovative ideas and new ways to live, think, and learn, and have even gotten the chance to start doing something I've always dreamed of, book editing.

My entrepreneurship journey has happened incredibly quickly. It was 3 months almost to the day from getting my first big project to quitting my full-time day job. I'm still navigating and figuring some things out, and I'm sure I'll make more missteps.

But I'm a business owner, and that is all a part of the process. Making mistakes, identifying and learning from them, and correcting them is a continuous process. The important things, like being a good writer, bringing value to clients, and being absolutely easy to work, with were what I had from day one.

But before I even got to the point of being a business owner, I had already started building it, without even knowing. Like I said, I've always been a writer.

As a profitable freelance writer and editor, people ask me questions all the time about **where I find clients and how much money I make**. I actually don't mind answering these because I think there is plenty of work out there and if you want to be a writer, then go for it! I love meeting other writers and editors; we can refer work to each other and commiserate and problem solve together.

It was 90 days almost to the day from getting my first "yes" from a client paying me to write until my last full-time day of work as a Business Development Manager at a staffing firm in Manhattan.

I now work from home with my cat as my fluffy, apathetic, and inquisitive coworker.

90 days.

3 months to change my life.

Chapter 2:
The Beginning

I fell into sales by accident at 20 years old, after graduating from the University of Florida with a Bachelor's degree in Anthropology. I applied to an HR position at a small publishing company in Gainesville, Florida, and they called me in for an interview!

While I was waiting for my interviewer, I saw someone I vaguely knew, and we stood chatting in the hallway. The Sales Manager came down the hall and told us to get back to work, and in my typical, 20-year-old snarky fashion, I joked about not working there and him not being my boss, so he couldn't tell me what to do.

He pulled me into his office, and we just talked for a while. He asked about my life and college, told me about his daughters, and we joked around. When the HR Manager eventually came looking for me for my original interview, Peter told her to hire me for his team, and I was to start immediately.

I accepted, and started my sales journey. It turns out that I am a natural at sales. I can talk to anyone, I genuinely like people, and people seem to like talking to me. I was consistently in the top three sales rankings every week, and was having fun. In the time in this role, I learned so much about myself, about professionalism, sales, technical writing, training, and other professional skills. This job was interesting, diverse, and gave me my first taste of leadership.

At 23, I decided to move to New York City. I only had experience in sales, so that is the job I looked for and was offered, and I have now been living in Brooklyn for over seven years. I didn't know anyone here at that time, but six months after moving, I met the man who is now my husband. He and I are so very different, but we are both funny, strange, passionate, and kind. We dated for five years, got married, and are continuing to annoy each other every single day.

I didn't choose the sales life; the sales life chose me. Each time I switched jobs, it was always a more interesting, better paying sales role. Even when I moved into staffing, and my dear friend Dan gave me a shot and hired me to be a Recruiter at his company, within six months, I was in a Business Development role again! My mom likes to joke that no matter where I go, no matter what I do, I'll always end up in sales. So far, she is not wrong!

Ten years after that first interview, I was still in sales. I was losing the love of closing the deal, things felt very repetitive, and I just wasn't feeling fulfilled anymore. I was still working hard and being successful, but wanted something more.

Over the years, many people reached out to ask me to edit an academic paper, help them write and edit their resumes and cover letters, and talk about blogging. I have written sales training programs for various jobs, written blogs and marketing content for different companies I've worked for, and I finally started to wonder if I could capitalize on that.

I'd started my blog in June 2011. I didn't really promote it much, just posted the links on Facebook. I think I somehow imagined that if I were funny enough, or posted often enough, I would magically get discovered and become famous and be offered a publishing deal.

I wasn't driving traffic to it, I just enjoyed it. I still do! But I wanted people to read my writing, and I knew I needed something more. To be honest, other than posting the links on Facebook or Twitter, I didn't even know how to drive traffic anywhere.

So, in 2015, I started researching different online publications and how to submit stories and articles, I applied to be a contributing writer for *Lifehack,* and they read my writing samples and accepted me! I spent a few months writing those, and even had a couple which were shared a LOT. My most-shared article is about weighted blankets helping with anxiety and insomnia and has been shared over 382,800 times since it was posted in January 2016, and I still sometimes get people emailing me about it.

Lifehack specifically gave article titles and instructions for distinct types of articles, such as lists of recipes featuring a specific food or for a type of event, or tips and tricks for productivity/organization, etc. Though they now allow you to suggest topics and write more of what you want, at the time it felt somewhat restrictive and frustrating to be so limited.

In mid-2016, I was approached in a semi-creepy way by an almost-stranger about possibly purchasing an invitation to contribute to *Huffington Post* for $150. *Huffington Post* (HP) editors each have invitations to their blogging/contributor platform, and apparently some sell their extra invitations.

Instead of purchasing it, I decided to do more research and actually found another way: I emailed Arianna Huffington directly and asked if I could write for her and attached writing samples. *[Please note that Arianna Huffington has stepped down as Editor-in-Chief and no longer runs the day-to-day operations at Huffington Post.]*

She responded within 24 hours with a link to an invitation and to create an account! I started writing posts for them immediately, and several got promoted by HP editors, which made me searchable and archived on the site.

Being able to write articles and post on Huffington Post was my greatest writing accomplishment to date! I was ecstatic, and wrote many posts over the next few months. When the editors promoted the posts by sharing them on social media, it allowed for a larger readership and more exposure. It was also personally very exciting to say I contributed to *Huffington Post*.

This was the first time I really started thinking about truly being a writer. I had always thought of myself as someone who wrote. Just like I'm a person who sings, though I'm not a singer.

This all happened before I even dreamed I could be a full-time writer and make a living with writing. I didn't think about it leading to a career yet, I just kept thinking it would be great to have more exposure for my name and my writing. I wanted it to somehow lead to a career as a writer, but I wasn't yet able to see ahead as to how that might happen.

But what these articles were really doing was allowing me to have published work and easy-to-access writing samples which I would eventually give to prospective clients.

I was enjoying my time writing and contributing articles to online publications, and seeing my name out there in the world. I even had a few people tweet at me and share my articles. Complete strangers! It was an amazing and gratifying feeling to see that people not only read my work, but also liked it enough to share with others!

I was honestly very happy with the way everything was going. I wasn't writing articles with the intention of quitting my job, I just wanted to write articles and get exposure and maybe get noticed and be able to write a book someday. I've always wanted to write a book, and I have several lists of ideas for different types of stories, including a really neat trilogy of a not-so-distant dystopian future.

I sat at work one day in my cubicle on Madison Avenue, which looked identical to my cubicle at my last job on Fifth Avenue, doing the same thing I did everyday: selling someone else's services.

I had been working in the staffing industry for over four years, selling staffing services to companies all over the country, working with clients and candidates to find the right person for the right job, writing and editing resumes and cover letters, leading sales trainings, and doing account management.

I didn't completely dislike my job, and I was very good at it. I made decent money and I loved my boss and my colleagues. Something was certainly missing; I didn't have the deep and abiding passion I wanted to have for my job or that my husband has for his, but I worked with great people who challenged me and made me laugh.

I didn't hate it, I just didn't love it.

In October 2016, I started using my research and sales skills and reaching out to people. A few days later, on Monday, October 31, 2016, I got my first paying client! I actually got TWO clients that day and two more on that Wednesday! Only three days in, and I had four paying clients!

My first few clients did not know they were my first few clients. I am extremely confident in my writing skills, so they could just judge me on that and my results, not on my relative inexperience. I had a website copywriting client, a press release client, a blogging client, and an editing client. In less than a week!

As soon as I realized it was a viable idea, and people really would sign a contract and pay me to write and edit for them, I immediately decided to go for it 100%.

Friday, January 27, 2017 was my last full-time day at my corporate sales job. Being able to focus more time on my business, I saw immediate growth and started to work through some of the challenges working from home really brings. It was 3 months almost to the day from getting my first client!

Chapter 3:
Say Yes to New Opportunities

B eing an entrepreneur is a constant lesson in things I don't know. It has truly been a valuable learning experience!

You don't have to know everything or understand exactly how everything in business works before starting a business. Guess what? I had no idea how to track expenses, do invoicing, or put together a contract that covered my client's and my own interests. I wasn't clear on exactly how much to save for income tax, or what type of business I qualified as. I didn't have a website or prices or anything!

I figured it out. So will you, because it isn't necessary to know all of those things right at the beginning. They're important, and you should research them and find the answers, but you'll figure it out as you go. It's more important to know HOW to find an answer than it is to just have all the answers.

You can research and learn what an LLC versus an S-Corp versus a sole proprietorship is, and how to become any of them. You can read and understand contracts and find ones that work for you; you can get templates and tax services and invoicing services online in many places. If you want any information, it's out there, you just have to go get it.

I chose to pay the fees and file as an LLC. I didn't have to, and it cost me about $1000 to do it, because New York is one of the few states that require you to publish your legal filing in a daily and a weekly newspaper for six weeks, paying the cost of those ads to the papers, and then pay a $50 fee to tell the state that you did the publishing for those six weeks. They even tell you specifically in which papers to publish!

Filing as an LLC doesn't change anything for my business or pricing, or how I do my taxes. I am a sole-member LLC, meaning I am the only employee, and because of that I am taxed as an individual still, not as a company. Which is great, as that makes it easier for me!

The reason I chose to file that way is because I'm married, and my husband and I have personal assets. As an LLC, if anything were to ever happen (G-d forbid!), only my business assets and accounts could be affected, not our personal ones.

More important than any filings or contracts, most important, really, is whether or not your idea/talent/skill/expertise is a viable business idea.

Before pouring money into advertising, marketing, sales funnels, legal filings, anything, you need to make sure what you want to do is a good business idea. Will people pay you for it? Will they feel they are getting a valuable service? What specific type of people will pay for your skills?

Understanding your audience and your market and what people will pay for is vital information when starting a business. If you are a writer or a business coach or a web designer, know there are a lot of those, everywhere. So, your questions should be whether the market can sustain another one, and how will you make yourself stand out from the others? What value do you bring no one else has? What is your specific shining skill?

The best way to find which ideas are viable is to start asking questions. Talk to people in your profession, ask advice. Ask them their pain points, their challenges, and any advice they have for a new person in the industry.

Also, find people who may need your services and ask them questions. For example, if you are a sales person and are looking to be a sales consultant, find people on LinkedIn, in real life, friends of friends, whomever, who own or are executives in small to midsize businesses, and ask if they would pay for your services.

Do some research and present it to them as a sales pitch. "I looked at your website, and I saw you don't have a blog or any social media other than a LinkedIn page. Would you pay for blogging and/or social media management?" See what they say, ask questions about what they need help with. It can help you with what services are needed in your market, you can start making connections and introduce yourself, and their answers can even help you set your prices.

This is called market research. You want to have specific questions ready and know what information you're looking for before you call them. And then make your call and be confident, listen, and make sure that you are asking the questions that allow you to guide the conversation and really dig to get the information you need.

This exercise often results in new clients, too!

The most important part of a business is being profitable. You can spend all the time in the world making your website look just right, but if you don't have any clients and no money coming in, then you've basically wasted your time.

Proving you have a viable business is essential. The way I did this was to just jump in.

When I got my first four clients the first week, I didn't have a website, set prices, contracts, processes, nothing. I had some writing samples (I used pieces I'd written and posted on LinkedIn, one from *Huffington Post*, and one from *Lifehack),* and I had enough confidence to blindly reach out to people and say, "Hi, I'm a writer. Do you need anything written? Here are a few things I've written previously."

As a writer, one piece of advice I saw everywhere was to create a niche for yourself. Beginning freelance writers are constantly being told to specialize in one specific niche, write samples and then search for clients within that niche, whether it is technology, academia, fashion, beauty, entrepreneurship, whatever it is, and become an expert, and then you'll find work by marketing your services only to those people within that niche industry.

That isn't bad advice. Being an expert in something specific and demonstrable allows you to easily create and prove value, charge higher - premium - prices, and really settle into one subject matter, as well as making it easier to find and get new clients. I've seen it work really effectively.

I know someone who is an expert at Search Engine Optimization (SEO), and he goes to small and midsize businesses which either don't have blogs or aren't ranking on Google's first page and says "Hi, I saw that you are currently ranked XY, and I can raise you up to Z by the end of the month. I'm a certified SEO Specialist, and here are three companies I've worked for that started at X and are now at Y."

He gets almost every client he speaks to, because he has very specific skills, and he knows exactly how to research and present his findings to new prospects.

I've seen similar success with people who wrote specifically for the legal sector, working for law firms, building their blogs and technical papers.

I did not go that route. I figured with my sales and marketing experience, I could have a wide reach, and I didn't want to limit who I would market to. I had some ideas on what I was going to aim for, but I decided to be openminded.

I decided to open myself up to new opportunities. **I simply said, "yes."**

I went out looking for clients and when asked if I did website copywriting, I said, yes. When asked if I could manage social media, I said, yes. When asked if I could create a website architecture, I said, yes.

When asked if I knew how to edit books, and later if I knew how to write a book, I said, yes.

If I wasn't completely sure how to do something, I did some research. I figured it out and I learned. There is so much information out there in the world, there is always a way to learn what you aren't quite sure of.

When I met a comic book publisher who asked if I had ever written a comic book, I said, "Not yet; I would definitely be good at it, though!" And he loved my attitude.

Now I am writing a comic book! An amazing opportunity I was open to, but likely wouldn't have thought of on my own.

I hadn't done ghostwriting before, now I have and it's become a major part of my business. Same with book editing. I love the books I get to work on, the authors I work with, and I even get to see the publishing process from the inside.

Every yes has opened a new door, taught me new skills, and continued to grow my love for what I do.

The variety and diversity of clients, projects, work, and types of writing I do keeps every day interesting and different.

I've turned down work I didn't want to do, or clients I did not click with. It's not about saying yes to everything, no matter what. It's about being open to new opportunities and not being afraid to try something completely new even when you are starting a brand-new business.

Saying yes can feel strange when you aren't 100% sure whether you can accomplish something, but you must be confident in yourself and your skills, and know what you can tackle and learn. When you're confident in yourself, saying yes to new opportunities is exciting, not scary.

Getting Started:
When I wanted to start a new business and find clients, I didn't have a lot of knowledge about how to be an entrepreneur, or how to go from blogger to paid writer. But I did have some specific skills and abilities which really helped me in this journey.

Sales, marketing, and business development experience have given me a deep understanding and ability to talk to people at every level and never feel intimidated by C-level executives or superior to any receptionists. I am comfortable cold-calling, answering objections, and not taking a "no" personally.

Other skills I have learned include closing deals, selling myself and the service or product, organizational and procedural training and experience, knowledge of how to use different types of business hardware and software, how to quantify sales and sales activities, creating, assigning, and measuring using metrics, how to forecast potential earnings for the next quarter, determining sales cycles, and other aspects of business.

I'm trustworthy and have countless proven track records and successful business relationships and have trained numerous employees.

Writing them out like this almost makes me feel impressed by my own skills! Really, though, I have worked at four corporations of different sizes, in different industries, in two different cities, and I learned. I paid attention to great and not-so-great management, training, how the businesses were run, what made employees happy (and unhappy), what made customers buy, and anything else I was exposed to.

Just because I never really thought too much about being an entrepreneur, doesn't mean I hadn't thought about growth and career advancement. Independence and ambition have long been at my core. Being great is important to me, somewhat because I want to live up to the expectations I imagine my family has for me, and expectations I have for myself. I have always been smart, or so I was told, and I want to live up to that, too.

But when it comes to business, my superpower is **relationship building.** I've spent the last 10 years building relationships with people in every level of business, from law firms, to insurance companies, technology startups, think tanks, universities, and more. I am great at building a relationship which transcends just business, over the phone, in emails, and in-person. I've known many of my clients' kids' names, pets, their lives outside of work. I learned to anticipate clients' needs.

I'm a good speaker, and I can talk to people about almost anything; I listen and ask questions. I must have a trustworthy face because people are constantly telling me things. Secrets about themselves, from the cashier at the grocery store, company gossip from previous colleagues and clients, personal relationship information, and more. I've become real-life friends with many of my clients! I tend to do well at networking events.

I love to talk and I genuinely like people, so sales has long been a fantastic fit for me, resulting in a solid career, great bosses, and progressive responsibilities.

The secret is that people seem to really understand I enjoy what I'm doing, so they react to me in the same way. I'm very informal and conversational on client calls, which is what works for me.

These skills allow me to flourish in my writing career.

Understanding what my skills are and how they can be applied was my first step in becoming an entrepreneur. You need to identify specifically what you are good at and what you need to learn, in order to go into this process with realistic expectations. For example, I am not particularly knowledgeable in accounting, and I chose to pay someone to do my business taxes this year instead of taking the time to learn how to do it.

Try to be aware of both your flaws and strengths. What can you do right now and what might you need help with? When you embark on a freelance and entrepreneurial career, you want to be honest with yourself. While I did say yes to new opportunities, they were all things I felt I could honestly accomplish.

I still said no to things which were completely out of my skillset. I was asked if I could design a website and I simply explained I had never really done that before and did not think I'd be good at it. I was asked to create a sales plan and strategy for a software as a service (SaaS) company, and I said no because I had never created one from scratch for SaaS and I did not want to spend my energy and time figuring out something that large and complex when it was not part of my core business.

You must learn your limits. I know what I'm good at and I also accept and acknowledge the things I'm not so great at doing.

I have also met some amazing people: other writers, editors, and other freelancers, like web developers and designers, all of whom I am happy to refer people to. It's been really cool to meet so many other entrepreneurs and share our stories and become friends and colleagues. I have had the pleasure of working with several of them on multiple projects, and I love it!

Chapter 4:
You are the Expert

So, how did it happen? What perfect storm brewed or stars aligned which let me go from working a full-time corporate sales job in a cubicle on Madison Avenue to working full-time at home in a hoodie, with my cat, in Brooklyn, in three months?

There were several steps I took. I used my specific skills to maximize results and tried to tailor what I needed to do with my abilities. When I couldn't use the skills I already had, I did research, asked questions, and figured it out.

First of all, sales and marketing, and I'll go much deeper into where my clients came from and how I made my first sales, as well as discuss best practices.

Secondly, taking advantage of social media marketing and knowing how important social media is these days to any growing business. I plan to dive into this further and talk about how I specifically used social media as a marketing tool without paying for any growth platforms. Social media is free, effective, and necessary for any entrepreneur.

Most importantly, I never told anyone they were my first, or second, or third client. I was an expert from the very beginning. If you aren't the expert, why are you starting a business based on that topic/ skill/ability? You must present yourself as the subject matter expert that you are from the beginning, not telling people they are your guinea pigs. No one wants to be anyone's guinea pig. They want to be confident in your abilities and know they are getting excellent value for their money.

That means you need to understand what you're doing, the process, and any numbers or statistics associated with it, and the major tools and software people use. Above all, you must be adaptable and willing to say, "You know, I'm not sure on that, let me get that information and get back to you."

Being an expert doesn't mean having all of the answers. **Being an expert means knowing how to find all of the answers.**

If you're looking for clients as a web developer, you need to be able to speak the lingo, even when you don't have all the answers. Same goes for other specialties, such as accounting. Any consulting or freelance work requires a certain amount of knowledge within that field, and the ability to do it well. Being able to talk about WHY people need an SEO expert, or how having a programmer offsite is directly beneficial to them, is how you sell yourself and your services.

I used all of my customer service skills to make sure I was and still am **responsive, available, and easy to work with**. I meet deadlines, ask questions when I'm unsure or need clarification, and I have made it my mission to be easy to work with. Clients want to work with people who are easy to work with. This is a must!

Think about it: if you make it easy to schedule time to work on something together, you always meet your deadlines, and are friendly, why would anyone not want to work with you?

The single biggest reason small businesses and entrepreneurs are successful, the reason they get and keep clients, is that simple. Be easy to work with and responsive to the clients' needs.

I have had prospective clients tell me they are going to give me a shot simply because I was available to jump on calls and continued to respond to emails quickly throughout their questions and concerns.

I've had current clients tell me I make their life easier and they never have to wonder if I'm making progress, because I always let them know what I'm doing for them and get things done when they ask.

I answer emails and texts even over the weekends, even just a quick acknowledgment like, "Yes, I see this and will take care of this on Monday. Thanks!" My clients don't have to hunt me down or wonder how long it will take to get an answer to their questions. During business hours, the answer is basically "immediately" and over the weekend or in the evenings, it might be a few hours.

This may sound like common sense, but you would be surprised how many people will say, "Well, I am only available from 8 am to noon. After that, I don't do meetings or calls." I am a sole proprietor, I don't quite have that luxury yet of turning down my client's available timeframes. I want people to enjoy working with me because I make the whole process easier. Of course, I still try to maintain general business hours, and I am always honest if something doesn't work for my schedule, but I simply offer alternative times.

Even if I did have the luxury of restrained timeframes, I don't think I would be that restrictive anyway. I enjoy speaking with my clients, and having our standing weekly meetings, which allow me to know exactly what is expected of me and what our team plans are for the week. I also work from home and like having the human interaction!

In fact, another aspect of being easy to work with is my requesting to have standing check in calls early each week. We talk about the previous week, upcoming goals and tasks, our progress, and often start working on the next project together, throwing around ideas. I really love the standing calls, as I feel like my goals, tasks, and expectations are set, and these calls really help me map out my week and my schedule.

Scheduling, prioritizing, and time management are extremely important when you are your own boss and working from home.

Despite my ready availability and striving to be easy to work with, I don't pander to clients. The customer is not always right. The customer knows what they want, but the expert knows what's possible. Instead of being a jerk about it, I simply say, "I completely understand, and that sounds great. Here is what I am able to do and why I cannot do exactly what you're asking. But I can get close!" And then explain it without a condescending attitude. If someone doesn't want to work with me, I don't take it personally. Just as in life, not everyone is going to like you. Not everyone is going to want to work with you.

I also did a ton of research throughout the process of finding and engaging clients. When anyone asked me what I charge for something, I did research to see what average prices for that particular thing was. Then I priced myself at the top of the bell curve, and sent them a proposal. Even at the very beginning, I tried not to price myself extremely low. Value often goes hand in hand with perception. Perceived value is just as important as actual value, as the perception is what gets the client in the door; then you prove your worth and continued value from that point on.

Some of the charts I worked from were definitely wrong, or I was looking at them incorrectly and my first few projects seemed like they didn't pay for my time at all, and I was making well under minimum wage!

But in November 2016, I just went right to work. I had four brand new clients. I spoke to each of them on the phone to discuss details of what they wanted, ask questions, introduce myself, and discuss prices. I followed up with emails reiterating our conversation, including pricing we discussed, the parameters of the project, and deliverables I would produce. I made myself available to chat if they needed, answered emails quickly, and started working immediately.

I set up folders for each client in Google Drive and had files for the proposal and notes from our conversations, the work in progress, out meeting notes, and anything else we need. As soon as I got home from work every day, I started working on these projects. I started making lists of what needed to get done and carrying that list in my purse at all times, so I could add to it or check things off throughout the day.

My amazing boss was kind enough and encouraging enough to allow me to take short calls during work hours. I would go sit in one of our closed interview rooms with a notepad and pen, and talk to clients when they needed a quick update.

I was working every evening until bedtime and all weekend long. I continued marketing and taking on more clients, finding new projects and articles to write, until I was so busy I could barely breathe.

I got another couple of clients.

And I loved it.

My husband and I sat down and discussed this possible business. It was only a couple of weeks in, but it looked like this was probably viable and it really might work, even though it hadn't been long.

Between my all-in passion for it, and the fact I proved so quickly people would pay for my skills, we took the idea seriously. Cautiously optimistic was how I was trying to think. It would have been easy to get excited really quickly. That's my typical way to jump into things. Wholeheartedly and super excited to dive in headfirst and do everything at once.

We had several in-depth discussions on plans, ideas, what entrepreneurship would look like for our family, for me, for our finances, and for our future. We had conversations surrounding money and what the income might look like. Some of this was hypothetical, but it had real applications.

For example, if we take someone who makes $60,000 per year, before taxes they make $5,000 per month. This seemed like a good salary to reach for, so my goal was to make $5,000 per month just from writing. We both understood the full amount might not be completely realistic with a full-time job, so we agreed that if I was getting paid half of that, $2,500 per month, then I would quit my job at that point and really make a full-time go of it.

I very conservatively and cautiously (probably for the only time ever) stated that within 12 months, I would quit my job and be a writer full-time.

In November 2016, still working full-time, I made $1895.

In December 2016, still working full-time, I made $1750, and signed my first 2 monthly retainer clients for long-term billing starting January 1st.

In January 2017, still working full-time, I earned $4088.72, and signed 4 more monthly clients.

My last full-time day at my office job was Friday, January 27, 2017.

By March, I had 10 clients, only one was not on a monthly retainer, and I did not have time for additional ones. **I had not spent one single dollar on advertising or marketing.**

Chapter 5:
Sales

Let's go deeper into the sales and business development, specifically some of the sales tactics I used, and how you can utilize them as well without needing years of sales experience behind you. I'm also going to go into detail about how to make the most effective cold calls.

Every single business in the entire world must have sales. Selling your product or service is how you make a living and bring in revenue.

Even if you say that you hate sales or you aren't good at it, too bad. You can hire people to sell for you, of course. But when you're starting a new business or you are a one-man show, then it falls to you.

Some people are afraid of sales, or feel uncomfortable asking people to spend money. My answer to that would be: how did you expect to make money in your business?

When you're first starting out, no one knows who you are. Do you think you can just exist and people will find you and hire you? That you would never need to do any self-promotion or sales?

Too bad!

Being able to sell yourself is important. How do you think the influencers in your field get and stay wealthy? By continuing to promote themselves and their brand. Getting to the top is one thing, but staying there is just as difficult, if not more so, because you have to keep proving yourself with more eyes on you.

But sales doesn't have to be so painful. A positive attitude makes a huge difference. In fact, it has been proven! When you're stressed out, your brain releases cortisol and adrenaline, triggering a fight or flight response, which can take a while to come down from and can be hard on your physical and mental health if you are stressed often.

Because the stress response starts with the hormones being released in your brain, scientists have been researching how the perception of stressful activities affects our response. The simple and most effective way to relieve stress is to change the view from one of stress to something else. An example *Psychology Today* gave was seeing certain experiences, such as final exams, as demanding rather than ominous or life-altering, kept people from feeling the negative effects of stress and still keeping their focus and fast information processing. Changing your mindset directly affects your brain's response to situations.

There you have it. Mindset and a positive attitude make a difference in life and even in your brain's responses!

How much money will you make when you go from "I hate sales!" to "I bet I can get two new clients this week!"?

I blogged for over 5 years, hoping someone would magically find me and fall in love with my writing and want me to write a book. I'm not sure why I expected that. Maybe it's those stories you hear of a web comic blowing up and getting a book deal or the way you hear of 15-year-olds being discovered at the mall. The idea you can just go about your daily life and somehow someone plucks you out of obscurity and you become something more. I'm sure it will be no surprise I loved the movie *Annie* as a kid!

So, sales.

First of all, be genuine. People don't like being aggressively sold to. When you're on a sales call, have a normal human conversation, introduce yourself and your company, but mostly just ask questions, listen to their answers, and be real. Don't just be thinking about what you want to say next, or following a script. Listen to the person, figure out what they need or if they have a need. Listen to how they answer your questions.

Honesty and being genuine really come through to people. They can tell when you're faking, and they will be turned off, but when you're just being yourself and having a conversation, they can see who you are. You will immediately come off as more trustworthy and not "salesy."

To be a good salesperson, you have to be able to sell yourself. Confidence is extremely important. If you aren't confident in your skills and abilities, why are you building a business around them? But there is always a fine line between confidence and cocky.

Walk that line carefully and don't cross into arrogance. Arrogance can come across as condescending when you're selling yourself to people.

In sales and marketing, self-promotion is required. If you have a problem with promoting yourself, then you may need to find ways which feel comfortable for you, like only emailing and messaging potential clients. But realistically, there has to be an element of self-promotion when you're trying to convince someone to pay you for your services. Being confident in your skills and how you can help their organization is still self-promoting, even if you don't think of it as such.

An effective cold call includes an introduction, a snappy elevator pitch, and either a call to action or a follow up action. First, you have to determine your goals for the call. Are you looking to make an immediate sale? Are you attempting to set an in-person meeting? Are you trying to give them additional information and set up a follow up call? Maybe you're looking for additional contact information? You could be looking for more information about their organization and their challenges.

Once you know what your goals are, you can reverse engineer your sales and marketing plans.

For example, if your goal is to have an in-person meeting with this person, then you should already know where their offices are. When you're on the call, after you've discussed your services and found out they have a need, say something like this:

"I would love to put a face to a name and talk further about this. I'll be downtown on Thursday; are you available at 2 or 3 for me to drop in and shake your hand?"

As soon as they say a time, I immediately respond with, *"Great! I will be over at 123 Main Street, 8th Floor, on Thursday, May 18th, at 2 pm. What's your email? I'll send you a calendar invite confirming this."*

Now I have their confirmed location, a time and date for meeting, their email address, and space on their calendar.

When you are asking to meet someone, always give a specific day or date, and then the choice of a couple of times. Psychologically speaking, people are more likely to say yes when they have a specific date focused in their minds, and can make a smaller choice, such as the time of day. They still feel like they are somewhat in control. But when you ask open-ended questions like, "Would you want to meet with me sometime?" It is easy to say "yes" and never follow up, or just not answer the phone when you try to call back.

My approach would be different if the goal were to make the sale and close the deal in one call. Then, instead of discussing a meeting, I would answer all of their questions, joke around and have a conversation, and end with something like this to close the deal:

"So, today is the 15th. Let's start working immediately and I'll only charge you for half of this month. I know we're putting together weekly blogs. Have you thought about a topic for this week and next week, or would you like me to come up with a few and you can pick from those?"

Again, I am assuming they already do want to work with me, and then I proceed to speak as if it's already a done deal and discuss details of the work, making sure to give them a choice to make. Again, it allows people to still have a measure of control, while being more likely to agree to the larger circumstance.

If it is a first call with a prospective client, then my goals are to learn and to educate. I want to learn about their challenges and their pain points, and educate them as to how I can solve those problems, with examples of their issues I can solve, such as, *"I understand you're having trouble getting blogs out weekly, and it's taking more time than you'd thought, and I can streamline the process and write the weekly blogs for you."*

Or I might be sharing more broad examples, *"Getting new and relevant content out regularly will raise your Google rankings and people will find you more easily. We can also share it on social media and continue to boost your exposure."*

Your approach and your conversation should depend on your goals. Your goals should depend on your business's goals and its' current needs. Are you looking to build up your monthly long-term clients, looking only for project clients, or are you in growth mode? There are different approaches for every possibility, as well as for each person or company you're reaching out to.

Your choice of people to call should not be random, but targeted to fulfill your own needs and theirs.

Sales is not random, nor should you think of it as so. All that you do in sales and business development should be for a specific purpose, whether it is to close a sale, educate a prospect, gather information, or grow your network.

Sales is about people. People can be predictable; they can be understood, they can be confusing, interesting, and fun. I love talking to new people. Everyone has a story, and there is something to learn from everyone we come across.

Sales is a learned skill, and can be taught. Anyone can become a good salesperson. But the best salespeople are the ones who have the right personality; the ones who can talk to a brick wall, see silver linings, and who can hear a no from a prospect without taking it personally. They shake it off and move right on to the next prospect, because every call, every handshake is a potential yes.

Though technology continues to evolve, cold calling and cold reach outs through email and social media remain a huge part of sales. After all, how can you continue to grow if you aren't finding people who are not already working with you or using your product? This is new business development, and even the largest companies in the world have teams of people doing it. I was one of them!

Every salesperson I know still habitually does cold calling. Most of them actually enjoy it! I always liked cold calling because I enjoy meeting new people, and I love a good challenge. Let's talk specifics of how to have the ultimate cold call.

10 Tips for Effective Cold Calls:

1. **Confidence** in yourself, **passion** in what you're selling, and being **genuine** are the keys to being great at sales in general and cold calling specifically.
2. **Background research**. Who are you calling and why/how would they benefit from working with you and your company?
   a. Check their LinkedIn page and their company's website. Get a feel for their products and services, and see what they are doing. Are they in the news a lot? Maybe you read they do a lot of volunteer work with a specific organization.
   b. These are things you can reference on a call with them. Just like in a job interview, you want them to know you are prepared and want to work with them and their company **specifically**; you aren't just looking for anyone who will say yes.
3. **Never apologize for calling someone**. You have a valuable service/product, and are giving them information which will

help their business, so you have nothing for which to apologize. "I'm sorry for calling you out of the blue like this, but let me tell you about my company..." No! Just start introducing yourself.

    a. "Hi, my name is Jyssica Schwartz, and I'm a writer and editor. Have you ever thought about writing a book?"

    b. "Hi, I noticed that you are an avid blogger and am wondering if you've thought about publishing your work?"

4. **Be deliberate in your reasons for calling**.

    a. "I saw you have not updated your blog in two months and I wanted to see what your plans are for content marketing?"

    b. "I checked out your company and could not find any Instagram, Twitter, or Facebook page for you. Are you looking to join social media to promote your business?"

5. **Remember: WIIFM: "What's in it for me?"** A prospect doesn't have to use your service, so your goal is to convince them they should.

    a. You're more likely to get a call back from someone, or for them to listen to you on a cold call when you have something which will directly benefit them. What can YOU do for THEM? This is how you should be approaching every call.

    b. How does your service or product **make their lives easier, save them money, generate money for them, or save them time?**

6. **You are selling yourself first.** You are a resource and an expert, and you're selling your company's services/products **second.**

    a. In order to do this, you need to be **professional, personable, and knowledgeable.**

    b. Your contact needs to be able to trust you and believe you know what you're talking about.

7. **You are the expert.** Ask the tough questions. Many people are uncomfortable asking about money and budgets and revenue in an initial call. But you need to learn more about this person

and their company and its specific needs, and asking different questions to be able to determine if they will directly benefit from working with your company.

   a. A big part of being professional is having the knowledge and training and ability to find out how you can directly benefit the person you're speaking to, as well as the company as a whole.
   b. You want this person on your side. Even if they are not the ultimate decision maker or check writer, having an advocate inside the company recommending you and understanding how your products and services would be good for them is invaluable.
   c. Part of being knowledgeable is knowing how to dig in and find out the right information.

8. **Stay in control of the conversation**. Not aggressive control, but guiding the conversation by asking the right questions and showing how your products or services answer their objections or address their pain points is important.

   a. This is another aspect of being knowledgeable and trustworthy.
   b. You're finding pain points and challenges by probing the right areas and you're making them really think about how you can address them and solve those issues, making their life easier and probably saving them time or money.

9. **Active listening** is especially important in a sales call. This is when you listen to what someone is saying in full, without interrupting, then paraphrase what they said ("So, what you're saying is…"), and then addressing any issues or concerns.

   a. The worst mistake salespeople make is having a script they refuse to move away from. People notice when you're just waiting for them to stop talking so that it's your turn again.
   b. This is a huge turnoff and your contact will not be able to trust you have their best interests in mind.

  c. If someone tells you, "I just don't think we can afford a blogger right now." You should never just say okay and move to the next question. You should be immediately responding, *"I understand you don't think you can afford it. Let's address this. If you had an active blog and better SEO and your site was higher in search rankings, you could be looking at a 20-40% rise in people seeing your site. We could also be doing targeted advertising and sharing on social media. If you were seeing those types of numbers 90 days from now, would a blogger have been worth it?"* **I repeated their objection back to them, and then gave a scenario where they couldn't NOT afford it.**

10. **Try different approaches**. Are you more casual or more formal? Which one brings you the most new contacts, the best conversations, the most information?

  a. I happen to be more informal and conversational with prospects, from CEOs to receptionists. That is what works for me and fits my style, and has generated the best return on my time and energy investment. I tend to say "hey" and use first names, no matter the title or rank.

  b. You may find that you are more formal, using Mr. and Ms. and not engaging in much small talk.

  c. No way is the "right" way of speaking to someone, it's simply what works best for you personally.

Also, make sure you're always taking notes when you're talking to prospective clients. You may not talk to them again for another week or three, so make sure that next time you call you are able to reference past conversations. Such as, *"Hi, Maria! I am just checking in. When we spoke two weeks ago you were just coming back from vacation and getting back to the grind! I have some ideas for you about possible topics..."*

I use a spreadsheet in Google docs to have contact names, email addresses, phone numbers, and notes on what we discussed, pricing, and other details. Find a way which works for you to keep track of all of your prospective clients. And no matter how great your memory is, don't ever just rely on that!

These are sales and cold call tactics I've used successfully and trained others on throughout my entire career in sales and business development. They should help you see how cold calling can be an effective tool in your sales arsenal, and show you how to can use cold calls as a way to drive business.

Chapter 6:
Marketing & Finding Clients

You want to make money from writing, and so did I. Here are a few ways you can start earning money quickly, as well as where I found my first few clients. I will chat a bit about blogging in the next chapter, which I use as a marketing tool, for exposure, and because I enjoy it.

Some of these are things I use and some I do not, but all are options. Other freelance writers I know have used some platforms I haven't and vice versa, but all of these options and many others exist for you to research and explore. You'll want to figure what works best for you.

If you aren't looking for larger clients and projects, or you aren't looking for them yet and just want to make money immediately, there are ways to do that. You can make money immediately as a freelancer, though it may not be great money, especially at first.

The easiest and cheapest way is content mills. Places like Upwork, ConstantContent, TextBroker, or Fiverr. Personally, I do not like these sites. Many people have had bad experiences; Upwork takes a 20% fee right off the top of your earnings, and I feel these perpetuate a lowest-bidder cycle for quantity, as opposed to paying fairly for high-quality work.

However, I freely admit I didn't use any of these very much, and Reddit and other forums have people who DID use these sites successfully with strict filtering to craft solid proposals, get well-paying jobs, and cultivate a long-term relationship with clients outside of the site, so it's really about finding what works best for you and doing some trial and error. Experiment! Use different writing samples, try different sites, and continue to use different platforms or websites to find where you're making money. I tried using Upwork briefly and was not happy with it, but I really didn't spend much time on it, either.

Make sure to do some research to see if these content mills are a good way for you to get started, and to also know what to expect. Some people use this as an opportunity to build a portfolio and are fine with the low pay, some are looking for the fastest way to start earning some money quickly, and others really have figured out how to use them to make decent money over a longer time.

In terms of being able to find immediate work and get paid, these types of sites can often seem like the easiest. They are free to join, you search for and send proposals for jobs, and if you get the job, you submit your work and get paid through the site. You can make yourself more attractive on these sites by taking and getting high marks on various skills assessments and having reviews from previous clients.

One way to find non-mill individual clients is to respond to and post free ads on Craigslist in the Jobs, Services, and Gigs sections, and on Reddit, in such forums as r/HireAWriter, r/Freelance, and r/ForHire (there are many more). Many people don't realize there are forums for everything on Reddit! I found one of my first clients on Reddit, in fact. He and I still work together on website information architecture and copy for the entire site whenever he has a new project.

Even when you're using a content mill or online forums to find work, you still have to sell yourself. You have to write and submit a proposal and writing samples, and then hope your proposal stands out from the rest. You want to be able to show people your value.

A top tip for selling yourself in proposals, pitches, and emails is to talk about THEM and the RESULTS they will see, not about you.

I am absolutely a victim of this, too. I forget to talk about their **needs** and what would be of **value**. I just want to tell them about my skills! This is something to be conscious of and it will make your pitch stand out from all of the others in a very positive way.

Most proposals say something along the lines of *"I am a writer with over 5 years of experience, and my niche is technology. Here are 3 writing samples which have been published on different technology sites and blogs. I would be a good fit for your project because… Here are my prices ____. Contact me at ____."*

If you want to really stand out and show your value to a prospective client, explain to them how working with you will directly benefit them.

"Your project sounds extremely interesting because… You need a further reach on social media, and to come up higher in the search rankings. The way to accomplish that is relevant; great-quality content marketing which is not just a random mashup of buzzwords and keywords. You should have informative, punchy content which will keep people on your site longer, give them better information, and encourage them to join your mailing list/buy from you/stay longer. You can get a stronger foothold and expand your reach using a combination of content marketing and social media management. Here is what I will do for you…"

Which pitch would you be more interested in?

Another way to make money with writing is to find websites which pay for articles. Personally, this is what I planned to do, but it can be tough, and many publications/blogs want new and original content, which means you would need to write a brand-new article and only submit it to one place, each of which can take 4-8 weeks to get back to you.

That takes a lot of time when you're just starting out, and a lot of effort for only one submission that may or may not be accepted and paid for. Then when I got busier and started making decent money,

I no longer had the time to craft individual pieces on the off chance it might get accepted to a publication, so I have not ended up going this direction yet.

Being a contributing writer to major publications and making a living is the dream for many writers, and one I share! I have written articles on *Lifehack, Huffington Post, Thrive Global,* and others, but these are not paid articles. I'd love to get into being a paid writer for *Entrepreneur, Forbes, Inc,* or any of the major blogs and publications; that would be so cool!

One of the main things stopping me is time, and also because I have seen the breakdown from some writers who write for *Mashable, Inc,* and *Entrepreneur.* One writer recently said she wrote over 140 articles in one month for various sites and had one of her first $5000 months. This is definitely impressive and very cool, but I am making the same money or more doing things completely differently, and writing far fewer individual articles per month. When she broke it down, it sounded like a lot of grinding and not very much pay per hour or per article, which is something you must consider.

I really don't know if that is typical, as I haven't been a paid writer for any of those publications yet, but hopefully someday!

I'll be going into pricing and value later, but the important thing to remember is that your time and skills are valuable and you deserve to be making a fair amount per hour once it all breaks down, not just a random dollar amount per article. You have to be charging enough to make fair hourly rates, in order to make sure it's worth your time and energy.

And then there is directly marketing yourself to companies and prospective clients. I have used this particular technique very successfully.

Direct marketing or direct sales is when you find a company you think you'd be a great fit for and you reach out directly to the company. You are not using a content website or a job board, you are talking specifically to the end client. No middlemen.

This works especially well when you have a niche or specialty you are targeting. The perfect example of this is my mom! My mom is retired and is also a professional editor, having edited books, resumes, and more, as well as spent 37 years as an English and reading teacher. If you're reading this, it's because she edited it for me!

My mom has experience with grant writing and fundraising and has been wanting to get more involved with those in her retirement. She is uncomfortable with job boards, like Craigslist and Indeed and has no desire to learn.

However, she is great over the phone and talking to people, as well as extremely personable and is able to sell herself without really trying. For her, direct marketing has been the best avenue for finding clients.

She finds midsize non-profit organizations in her area, looks them up online to see exactly what they do, and finds the Executive Director or Fundraising Manager, and reaches out to them to ask if they are interested in using a freelance grant writer or fundraiser. Not only is she more comfortable finding clients this way, because she is so specialized (non-profit grant writing), she is able to find companies to market herself to very easily.

If you are not specialized or have a specific niche, you can always just pick a topic you've written about more than once and shoot for those. If you've done product descriptions for one or two places, why not reach out to e-commerce companies you see have bad or no descriptions and offer your services? It may not be your overall specialty, but you have experience and that is a very specific area.

One way I have used direct marketing is to look for a company which specializes in human resources or recruiting. When I find one, I check their blog. If it is nonexistent or sparse I reach out to them. My message might look something like this:

Hello, I hope you're doing well! I was on your site today and noticed your blog has not been updated in over two months! I happen to be a freelancer writer, and my background is 10 years in sales and business development, the last 4.5 in staffing and recruiting agencies in NYC.

I am very interested in writing blogs for you, especially with your recent article in TechCrunch about how your software for visual resumes utilizing 3D modeling is changing the industry. Congratulations!

I'd love to talk to you about how regularly putting out new content will raise you even higher in the Google search rankings and I have a couple of ideas of how we can educate people on what a visual resume is and how it makes you stand out! Do you have 10 minutes to jump on a call to discuss?

Have a great day,

Jyssica

You want to personalize the email to show you're interested in working with them in particular and not just anyone, and say something which shows you went one step further than others do. You didn't just look at their homepage, but have some piece of relevant news or information about them. You can look at the media page of their website, search their company, and check for press releases for an announcement. Anything to show you're paying attention to them.

After I send this, the next goal is to schedule a time to talk at their convenience. On the call, I'll have 2-4 topics I think would be a good fit for their blog, and specifically discuss my pricing. Many companies genuinely want more active blog content and engagement with customers but are busy and just don't have time to do it themselves.

I often offer to do it at a one-blog cost, so they can see the quality of my writing, and I also offer to post it directly on their blog for them, as well as write them the short copy for a social media post about it.

Think about it. For one price, you get original content, a picture for the post, it gets posted to the website and then you only have to copy and paste a sentence and link to social media. And YOU get all the credit! Of course, it is a valuable service and useful to them!

When it comes to specific areas or industries, direct sales is incredibly potent and essential. It is such an amazing way to create your own clients. You are actively going after people as opposed to sitting there and waiting for people to magically find you.

Yes, you are cold calling, but these are qualified leads of companies and people who would genuinely be a good fit for your services. It's not like you're flying blind!

Chapter 7:
I Just Want More Clients

What if you already have a business and are looking to expand your service offerings or simply find new clients? Maybe you have a few clients but aren't making quite enough money, or you find yourself grinding and hustling, writing 25 articles each week for meager pay.

When I first met James Ranson, an incredible editor and writer, a friend, and the man behind the lovely and gracious foreword at the front of this book, he had been an editor for three years.

I'm not joking, he's an amazing editor, better than me. We all have our talents, and he found his early. Unfortunately, he wasn't making nearly as much money as he was certain he deserved, or finding the higher caliber of clients he wanted. He had a few, but wanted more.

But James also hated the idea of marketing. In a statement he wrote in 2015, James once proudly stated that "Marketing is like Japanese. It's a language I've never studied, and it has little or nothing to do with my work or daily life. It's so complex it would take years just to master the basics. I have no desire to learn it, and I can avoid ever needing it by simply never going to Japan. Breaking my head over learning marketing doesn't interest me, and I have better things to do with my time. I don't see why anyone would bother with marketing."

For James's sake, thank goodness he waited until after we became close friends before he showed me that!

After we'd known each other for about six months, James cracked. He had recently lost out on two potential clients and needed to find new ones. He came to me, metaphorical hat in virtual hand, to ask for my help with sales and marketing efforts. He claimed he saw the light, but I'm pretty sure he was just willing to humor me and be able to claim he tried everything when whatever my plan for him to try ultimately failed.

After all, he was an expert, what could I possibly do to change his business?

As soon as he asked, I made him pull up a document immediately. We had to do it NOW, in case he changed his mind. I know I can be annoying, too upbeat, and have too many ideas at once, but I am also really good at sales and finding clients. I jumped at the chance to show my friend what he was missing and how it could help him--WITHOUT it being overwhelming, frustrating, tedious, or futile. I could help him create a realistic step-by-step plan that made sense for him and his business.

Over the following 90 minutes, that document became James's marketing plan. It included exactly what his following four weeks would hold, with each step taking one week. It also included his expanded service offerings with new pricing and details, as well as his ideas for future plans.

For all he teased me about always having so many ideas and constantly thinking about "someday" instead of right now, James had also been thinking about his business future, and he had some great ideas for expansion of book coaching and working one-on-one with authors, and for adapting his editing packages for different people and genres.

So, we came up with a plan.

Step 1: Reach out to all previous clients and prospective clients from the past.
This required him to go dig up the email addresses of everyone and create a list, but once you do that the first time, it is done forever. You

can put them all in a spreadsheet or create a free MailChimp or other similar service account to set up a subscriber list.

The goal of step 1 is to now have an email list, let them know about the new service offerings and pricing, ask for referrals, and start a conversation. Previous clients and prospects are perfect examples of "low hanging fruit," the idea they will be easier to persuade to work with you since they already know who you are, than it will be to find brand new clients and start from scratch.

Step 2: Reach out to online publishers.
James already worked with 2-3 online publishing companies as an editor and ghostwriter, but the work isn't steady, it is project work. It seemed like minimum effort for a potentially large reward to reach out to other similar publishers and offer himself as a freelance editor and ghostwriter who they can recommend to their clients.

The main goal of step 2 is to think about how to do more with what you're already doing well. If you already have a successful avenue of business and income, reaching out to similar companies and offering the same service makes perfect sense.

Step 3: Flesh out new (and current) service offerings.
James put together a list of everything he offered, and clarified what each service included and how much it cost. He also decided to add content marketing/blogging to his service offerings. He had already been doing it on a small scale, but when he looked at how I structured my content clients, and thought about the time versus money tradeoff involved, it really made sense for him to be offering that on a larger scale. James already had a strong track record of working with thought leaders in different industries to create content. He then started researching and strategizing around who to market these services to, and how to find them.

The goal of step 3 was to finish fleshing out exactly what he would be offering, the pricing, what that would involve in terms of time and effort, and then start marketing that to companies which could use those services.

Step 4: Work on and expand his online presence.
Because he already had a successful freelancing business, James had not been too concerned about creating and maintaining an updated online presence. His last step would be to start writing blog posts again, clean up his website, start getting involved in online writing websites and forums, and refine his LinkedIn profile and website to reflect his current services and business. This step also would include (after the initial four weeks) writing and launching the two or three books he'd been planning on writing for years but hadn't done yet.

The goal of this step is to really create a presence online and to think about the future and not just the present state of your business. People like to work with people they can trust and feel like they know. Seeing your LinkedIn page and website is great, but finding you on Twitter or Instagram, or seeing you answer professional questions on Quora or your blog will reinforce that you are a real and entire person outside of just writing, and will reinforce that you are who you say you are and that you are trustworthy.

James jumped on board. He said that he had nothing to lose by trying and would make a genuine effort to follow the plan - which he did, even though the steps ended up taking longer than a week each. I made him a wager that he would have new clients in two weeks regardless.

I won that bet.

Since then, James has become somewhat addicted to answering Quora questions, has been actively blogging on Medium, and has gained interest from brand new avenues he hadn't considered (and he's admitted that yes, there is value in marketing!).

Last chapter showed five ways you can find clients when you're building a brand new freelance business, and so far in this one, how a marketing plan helped an established freelancer expand his existing business.

Where did my first few clients come from?

My First Four Clients

You do not need a portfolio before getting clients. I see people all the time taking work for little or no money "for the exposure" or to build their portfolio. Stop it. Stop it right now. Your skills are worth money, your time is worth money. Stop assuming that just because you have no professional experience you must work for nothing.

Write three articles you're proud of. They can be about anything. Three on similar topics but different points of view, three completely different topics, or you can write something very specialized. It doesn't matter what you write about unless you're going for a very niche industry. Just write them and use them as writing samples. Don't tell anyone they are your first client. When they look for experienced writers, if you have the skills and the knowledge to write for them, just say *"Hi, I'm a writer. I can definitely do XYZ. Here are a couple of writing samples."* You can post them to a blog (I have a Blogspot, my website is a WordPress, and I actively use Medium and Google docs) or just save them as a PDF and email them when requested.

I got my first four clients in three days, and that was the actual beginning of my writing business. About a week before I got my first clients, I'd started posting ads, responding to a few, and reaching out to people. For writing samples, I used pieces which had been published on *Huffington Post* and *Lifehack*, and since those are both fairly recognizable names, it gave me some instant credibility. I also linked to my blog, since I had several different types of writing and tones in those posts, so it shows variety and diversity.

I have a couple thousand LinkedIn connections and people I've spoken with, sold to, or met over the years while in different jobs and industries. I've been to and even spoken at some industry networking events and trade shows, which served to give me additional exposure and added to my growing LinkedIn base. I also write articles on

LinkedIn using their publishing platform, and a few of them had several thousand views and great conversations in the comments. I felt confident in my exposure and being able to have conversations with people over LinkedIn.

So, my first attempt at finding clients was to write a short message and send it my contacts on LinkedIn. Not all of them, but specifically to people I had either had a personal friendship or prior working relationship with, and to all owners, founders, C-level executives, and directors of small and midsize companies. I also included content, digital, and marketing agencies in this list. I was careful not to send it to anyone I currently worked with, or to clients my employer was working with as I didn't want to have any conflicts of interest.

My note was very simple and not very personalized. I still maintain that personalizing your message it best, but I sent out a bunch and I was pasting the same message into all of them. Here it is:

Hello [First Name],

I hope you're doing well! I wanted to reach out because I have finally started living my dream of being a freelance writer. I love words, and you know that content is king and is what sets companies apart from their competition.

So, I am offering my services to the world. Content creation for your website, editing, articles and blog posts on request, creating new copy for your Google ads, email templates, writing press releases, and much more.

I have 10 years of professional sales experience, as well as writing experience across Huffington Post, Lifehack, LinkedIn, and others. I would love to work with you; please let me know if you have any questions or have time to jump on a call.

Have a great day!

Jyssica

My first client came from sending this LinkedIn message, and that first project turned into six months of monthly retainer work, and a great working relationship with a CEO of a consulting business.

Over time, I have not had a ton of ongoing success in finding new clients on LinkedIn, though I have continued using the Publisher and gotten more followers, and have had new clients and prospects find me and connect on LinkedIn, even if we met on other platforms. My marketing efforts adapt and change as everything moves forward.

Next, I went through Craigslist and Reddit and had a similar but shorter prepared message to send out in response to ads.

On Craigslist, there is an area for writing and editing under the "Jobs" section and listings for part time and temporary work there, as well as a writing and editing section under "Services." And because many writing and editing jobs are remote, you can look and find cities with more roles available or more variety. I posted free ads under "Services" and "Gigs," and was responding to ads under the "Jobs" section.

My second client came as a response to my ad on Craigslist. He is the owner of a small travel company in New York City and had a fairly small budget, but needed new copy for his website, Google ads, and landing pages. When we jumped on a phone call, we clicked immediately and he liked my ideas for his website. After completing the first project, we continued working together for the next three months, doing email templates for sales emails, copy for additional pages on his website, and putting together sales strategies and ideas.

On Reddit, you can respond to people who post looking for freelance writers, and you can also post an open ad with your experience and links to writing samples, so people can contact you directly. The three main subreddits I was looking at were r/HireAWriter, r/Freelance, and r/ForHire. My post discussed how my 10 years of sales experience really gave me the insight and ability to write well-suited-for-marketing content for websites and blogs, and I included links to a couple of writing samples.

This is how I got my third client! He had posted an ad looking for someone to write the copy for a website he was building, and I responded with a direct message. He owns a small web development company in New York City, and wanted someone to write a site architecture and copy for his newest website he was building. I jumped in and happily wrote all of the copy currently on his site. He is an entrepreneur himself, and loves working with freelance designers, developers, writers, and more.

He is definitely an idea guy, and since that first site, we've now worked together on three more websites he and his team have created!

My fourth client came from a direct sales message. I happened to come across a website for a small company in the Midwest whose main service was writing resumes and doing job searching and interview coaching. This seemed perfect for me, as I was still working for a staffing agency, and had been in staffing for over four years.

I reached out to the owner of the website directly. I told her that I loved her site and service, and noticed that her blog hadn't been updated in over three months, then suggested three topics that I could write blog posts about that would fit with her site, and asked if she was interested in hiring a blogger? She said that she loved my initiative, and while she wasn't looking for a blogger yet, she did want someone to write her a press release and discuss her backstory, business success, and new services. She didn't have time to do it, and said she would be happy to pay me.

I'd never written a press release (though I've written several since then!), so I looked up recent press releases to see their structure and what information they included. I was able to write it, and we left the door open for a possible relationship in the future.

I was using different client-finding sources and seeing what came from each. Over time, I've found what worked best and what didn't. For example, LinkedIn has not been great for finding new clients, but has been good for personal exposure and driving traffic to posts I've written on my website and on Medium. Reddit has been a great resource for information and having a community of other writers and freelancers, and being able to share stories, challenges, and triumphs, but is hit and miss when it comes to finding steady work. Most of my current clients are from referrals and directly marketing myself to business owners.

This is how I found my first four clients ever, and I've used these and other ways to get new clients since then. It's important to try different things to see what works, but don't be afraid to stop spending your time on things which are not giving you a decent rate of return. I no longer advertise my services in LinkedIn, but I do have my company and services listed on my profile.

It's important to think outside the box, and try as many different ways to get clients and promote yourself as possible. What worked best for me may or may not work best for you and your audience.

Surprisingly, what has ended up being the most effective and constant for me over time has been social media. In fact, after those first four clients, my next one, who has become a major client of mine to this day, came from Instagram!

Chapter 8:
Social Media Marketing & Blogging

Using social media is an integral part of continuing to build my business. Half of my clients came from Instagram, and at the time of this writing, my most recent client came from Twitter!

So, how am I using social media to my advantage? For one thing, I am actively sharing my new blogs and articles on social media and tagging them so they are being shown to as wide an audience as possible. I'm posting regularly and being an active member of Instagram and Twitter, and posting more than just my articles.

I post pictures of my life, such as my cat, when I travel, food I cooked, and more of my cat. I'm not just a random writer looking for exposure, I'm presenting a whole person with a life and interests outside of self-promotion.

I actively engage with others, following, liking, and replying to people. I try to post things which are interesting, and only use relevant tags so no one gets annoyed.

Whenever I get a like or comment or a new follower who has "CEO," "entrepreneur," "founder," "creator," "marketing," or "public figure" in their bio, I send them a quick note in a direct message.

My message is very straightforward:

Hi, my name is Jyssica Schwartz, and I am a writer and editor in NYC and am available for new projects immediately. Having 10 years in sales and business development means I write well-suited-for-marketing copy. Do you need any blogging, copywriting, press releases or other writing services? I also ghostwrite and edit books!

I'm a contributing writer to Huffington Post, Lifehack, and others, and can send you samples of my work.

I alternate between that type of message and something more enigmatic, like:

Have you ever thought about writing a book?

It's a great hook! And many people are intrigued. As I've tested it, I try to see who is responding to each type of message. Which are more effective to whom? I do book coaching, ghostwriting, and editing, so I can help from the beginning of the process.

I actually have a pretty high response rate from Instagram and Twitter. Many people ask questions about pricing and services and what I could specifically do for them and their business. If we are having a great conversation, I ask if they're available to jump on a phone call. I tend to do well over the phone, so I try to get people on a call as soon as possible.

When people first respond to my message, I check out their website (if listed) before answering, so that I can tailor my answers to their company.

If they have a clothing company, I can respond to them talking about how I can do product descriptions and ad copy. If they have a digital marketing agency, I talk about my blogging experience for different clients. If they say they have already written a book, I look it up to see what they wrote about and then discuss the topic and a possible second book.

One of the people who responded to one of my messages in December owns an online publishing platform and book marketing company. We ended up talking and collaborating on several projects. He is an entrepreneur himself and uses every opportunity to work with people who are building and creating their own businesses. A writer and published author, his company focuses on helping others get their work out into the world, including me with this book.

I started working here and there on different smaller projects for that publisher; the owner and I clicked, and really began a great working relationship and friendship. He introduced me to another writer and editor, who became a friend and someone to bounce ideas off and rant to. He has referred me to several other entrepreneurs looking for writing and editing help, and he gave me my first opportunity for book editing, something I have always wanted to do.

Instagram and Twitter were also successful for me with other clients. I found several more clients from those platforms, including weekly blogging clients in different industries, a couple of copywriting clients, and even authors looking for editors. I continue to gain followers and exposure even now on social media, and actively use it. I have not yet invested in any Instagram growth platforms, though I know I could grow my followers faster. Aside from buying my domain name and hosting my website (we already owned hosting services), I haven't put any money into getting clients and advertising services or growing social media.

As a side note, I have not been using Facebook as a work platform. Most of my friends and family don't live in the same state as me, and I use it mainly to keep in touch and share pictures with them. I haven't been using it as a place to really advertise my services. You can pick and choose what platforms work best for you. For me, having one that was only for personal use has been great, and gives me a place to see family and friends and their goings-on, without being inundated with work-related things.

Now, the majority of my current clients have come from either social media or referrals. As you grow your business, referrals and recommendations are the best possible way to get new clients. A satisfied customer is worth their weight in gold. It's also extremely gratifying to know people see the value in my work, so much so they are willing to recommend me to people they know, which means they are staking their reputation on me.

I am honored and flattered that most of my clients have been referred to me, and that I have strong, successful relationships with them. Some of my clients have become friends of mine in real life!

Though I am not actively marketing myself at the moment, I'm never *not* selling myself.

I continue to publish blog posts and articles, respond to publicity calls to be quoted in articles, and introduce myself and hand out my card when I meet people.

I made business cards on Vistaprint.com when I first started out, so I was able to have something physical to hand to people. Mine are vertical and black with red accents. I designed them myself and I love them. They include my email address and website, though not my phone number.

I also keep my website updated. It's a WordPress site with one of the free themes, and I was able to mess around with it and customize it to be something I am happy for people to see. Even though I don't advertise the site often (I give out my Medium blog a lot!), I make sure the blog is updated, the site is typo-free, the media page is updated with any publicity mentions, etc.

Funny enough, because no one would ever accuse me of being super technical, but the week I spent messing around with, building and customizing my WordPress site made me comfortable enough with it that most of my clients have given me the log ins to their websites and have asked me to post blogs or make changes to their sites! They seem to think I'm some sort of WordPress expert because I can update pages or add a widget!

Blogging.

I had to talk about blogging eventually!

Blogging is my one true love. I started this whole journey with my personal blog in 2011, which I updated regularly; it inspired me, frustrated me, and became a scrapbook of my growth through writing and my life changes. That blogging experience eventually led to me becoming a contributor *to Lifehack* and *Huffington Post,* which led me on the path to seeing if I really could get paid to be a writer. And here I am.

Even though I am now paid to write for other people, everything from blog posts, articles, bios, website copy, and entire books, it has not diminished my love of writing for myself.

I have switched to a new platform, Medium. It's a free blogging platform and I have found it to be wonderful. It's easy to use, it saves drafts automatically, and there are publications on it that pull their writers from regular Medium bloggers. I even started our own publication for my publishing client!

Now, when people want writing samples I just send them to my Medium account. I am a contributing writer to three different publications, *Thrive Global* (Arianna Huffington's project), *The Writing Cooperative,* and *Authors Unite.* I have been flagged by Medium as a "Top Writer" in the Entrepreneurship and Books categories, and I've been exposed to some amazing writers and content on Medium.

For me, I have had a very positive experience on Medium, and I'm glad to have found something which works for me both in giving me exposure and finding new writers to read. I have been regularly blogging and putting up content about writing, my business, entrepreneurship, anxiety, reading, and books. I enjoy it, and I was even able to include some of my blog content in this book (especially in chapters 9-11).

Blogging is still a big part of my life and writing, and I highly encourage anyone thinking about writing a book to try blogging. Many people put off writing a book because of time constraints. Blogging will allow you to be creative and produce new content, but in much smaller bites!

I've also found that because I know how long it takes me to write blog posts, that I was better able to gauge how long it would take me to write a book. I wanted about 30,000 words and I was able to estimate how many weeks it would take to write this book. I was surprisingly accurate!

I love blogging. I love the shorter content and the way I have to edit myself and be concise. I enjoy trying different writing styles, from storytelling to reporting. I like sharing my knowledge. Now that I'm a freelancer, I get a lot more questions about writing, the writing process, clients, pricing, and much more. Blogging is a fantastic way to continue to try to sell myself as an expert and share what I've learned.

Interestingly, the more often I write for my blog, the more inspired I am to continue writing and coming up with ideas. Creativity breeds continued creativity. Actively writing regularly keeps me inspired and fulfilled.

Chapter 9:
Value & Pricing

It is very easy to undervalue yourself. There are innumerable reasons. Maybe you want to use a low price point to bring people in, or you don't truly know the value of what you're doing yet, or someone once told you to charge XX amount, or maybe you did a bit of research and priced yourself on the lower side of average.

Pricing is the most difficult part of being an entrepreneur. It took me several months of trial and error and being paid much lower than I wanted to figure it out. Part of the reason it is so hard to price myself is because writing comes fairly easy to me. I mean, I'm good at it and people are willing to pay me, but it's not something which is hard for me to do, and often feels fairly easy. Because of that, I had very little knowledge of how difficult writing is for other people, which led me to undervalue my services at first. It has taken time for me to realize the value of the service I'm providing and raise my prices to a more competitive level!

Research, research, research. Do more of it. When you think you've done enough, look at a few more sources. Also, be sure you are calculating your time. If you are charging $0.05 per word for blog posts, and it takes you four hours to research, write, and edit that 1000-word post, then you got paid $50 for one post, but you are actually getting paid $12.50 per hour, which is not great, and is the number you want to be paying attention to.

Thinking about your pricing per hour will help you better decide on good prices, as you want to focus on the value of your **time** not your finished product. For example, you may get a client who wants a weekly blog post of 800-1000 words. You think about how long it takes you to write one post, let's use the four hours from before. You calculate that it will take you 16 hours per month to write those posts, and decide to charge the client $400 per month, putting you at $25 per hour.

This seems completely reasonable when you first look at it. But wait, there's more! You also need to consider the time it takes to come up with several post topics and discuss those with the client, before they pick the ones for that month. You need to add in time for meeting with the client to discuss ideas, posts, and processes, add in time for your client to look over the posts and for you to make their edits and revisions, the time it takes to post the blog to their website, including finding and adding relevant pictures. Add in time if they want you to promote their new blog post on their social media pages. In the end, you might spend 23 hours per month, which puts you at $17.39 per hour.

You must focus on your total time spent on each task and post, as that is how you want to be valuing yourself. Your time is valuable and is your main commodity. How much you want to be paid per hour is an important number to decide.

As I mentioned, value often goes hand in hand with perception. Perceived value is just as important, if not more so than "actual" value, as **perception is what gets the client in the door**, then you prove your worth and value at that point with the work you do.

This is why you have to price yourself competitively, even if your business has less overhead than your direct competitors. You may feel great at a certain lower price, but if your prospective clients are comparing your business to your competitors, they don't know or care about the reasons why, they just see you are priced at $1000, and your direct competitor is priced at $3500 for the exact same product or service.

Even if they think the other company is overpriced, they are going to ask themselves why you are SO MUCH cheaper. Is it lower quality?

Are you cutting corners? Are you lying about your results? Are you very inexperienced?

These are questions they will ask themselves, even if it is subconscious. The perception of your value is extremely important. Therefore you stay priced competitively and have testimonials up on your website.

Testimonials and having references is important. It's about credibility. One of the reasons I'm writing this book is to reinforce my credibility as a writer. And because as a ghostwriter, my name is not on the books I have helped to create. I want my name on the cover of at least one!

I want to touch on **contracts**. Many freelancers have had issues getting paid on time or even getting paid at all sometimes! I've been lucky that so far, I haven't had many issues and have wonderful clients who pay me promptly and don't dicker over each penny. I've had a few late payments, but talking to the client directly and honestly made those payments appear.

I believe the primary reason for this is because we have contracts in place. I had never had a contract for writing, so I looked online for examples and templates. I found a straightforward one I liked which spells out who the client and business are, the prices and exactly what deliverables, measurements, or results are included, and also has billing preferences.

For example, for a project I charge 25% up front and the rest on completion. But for monthly retainer clients, I don't charge an upfront cost. I send out invoices on or around the 20th of each month for the full monthly amount.

I did do some research on different invoicing and payment tools, and I went with PayPal. It's super easy to use, it's a free account with unlimited invoicing, and it just keeps it all streamlined. For me, a PayPal Business account was the simplest solution.

Having a contract in place makes everything more official and legally binding. Someone is signing it, promising to pay you and you have spelled out exactly what they can expect from you. **You should absolutely have a contract in place with each of your clients before beginning work.**

I have my own contract I use, and some of my clients prefer to use their own. That's fine, I just read it over and make sure it aligns with my goals as well. I have also had clients who require Non-Disclosure Agreements, which I am also happy to sign.

Having processes for qualifying new clients, discussing project specs, putting together a contract, and invoicing makes me feel like a real business. Contracts are in place to protect you and your interests as well as those of your clients. This is another value-add for potential clients, as they know I am the real deal.

Speaking of, how do I add value to my clients? What differentiates me from the thousands of freelance writers out there?

One way I add value to my relationships with my client is by being organized and an expert. On our initial calls to discuss working together, pricing, and scope of the work, I always talk about collaboration and flexibility, how we will work together, and what the end result will look like.

I have standing weekly meetings with *every single one* of my clients.

I am the one to request having a weekly call early in the week to discuss that week's work, the specific tasks either side needs to complete, and discuss ideas and plans. Having a weekly call ensures both sides are always completely clear on expectations, deadlines, and where we are in any given project. It also makes sure both sides are always happy with the relationship. If something needs to be addressed, there isn't time to let it grow and fester. When you talk every week, you are always able to reassess and make changes. It also continues to build the relationship.

This is yet another way I am bringing value to them; I clarify every week what I will be accomplishing, without them having to track me down or wonder when or if something is getting done. Every one of my clients has been happy with having a weekly meeting, and often invites other team members to join the call, so that we have weekly team meetings.

For my editing clients, I try to be the most collaborative editor possible. I like to edit their work in a Google doc they have access to. They can jump in and see my progress, ask questions, reply to any comments or questions I left, and really see their book coming together to become the final product.

Their book is their baby and part of their soul, and I have had very good responses to this way of editing. Instead of handing their book to an editor and not seeing it for 3-4 weeks, they are getting a front row seat to the entire editing process, and are able to make sure nothing massive is changing in their book.

For my ghostwriting clients, we have 1-2 weekly meetings to continue writing their books, blogs, or other things, while always making sure it is in their voice, their story, and allows the client to be in control of the story, the pace, and the editing.

Ghostwriting is something which is incredibly interesting and satisfying in a totally unexpected way. I didn't know anything about ghostwriting, really. If I thought about it at all, I just associated it with celebrities who put out books. It turns out that ghostwriting is a tool for anyone! If someone has a story to tell but neither the writing talent nor the time to put it together, then a ghostwriter is a perfect solution.

I've written several books now, though none under my name, which is part of the reason I wrote this one! Ghostwriting is a really neat process, too. One way to do it is to have several long interviews at the beginning of the process. Ask all the questions, start putting together the outline of the story, and get the recorded interviews transcribed.

Another way to do it is more collaborative and the author is involved a lot more. In our first couple of calls/weeks, we talk about the entire story and put together an outline for the book. It's all done in Google docs, so we both have access. The author reviews the outline and makes sure it makes sense for the story he wants to tell. Then each week, on our calls, the author tells me the next bit of the story, in much more detail. I can ask more questions and he elaborates. Afterwards, I write the next section or chapter, and the author goes in and reviews it and makes suggestions or changes. Often, he remembers a detail or edits something for accuracy. Then we move to the next section or chapter.

This process allows the author to be fully involved at every step in the writing of the book, but with a commitment of only 1-3 hours per week.

This has all been a work in progress. Like most business owners, I'm figuring things out as each situation crops up. But being fully aware of expectations and workflow, and what I need to be getting done every week really helps me with organization and prioritization, as well as keeps my clients happy, as they know exactly what I'll be delivering each week.

Of course, there are all kinds of challenges when you work where you live which I didn't really expect or anticipate.

Chapter 10:
Biggest Challenges So Far

Working from home presents its own challenges, from how simple it can be to sleep in or stay in pajamas all day, to how easy it can be to get distracted. Time management is an entirely new challenge, as well. You no longer have a manager to tell you what to do or give you specific parameters and deadlines or to guide you when you have questions.

Time management, prioritizing tasks, and staying focused on one thing at a time are still obstacles I am working on climbing over to this day. I try to stick with what works and also be willing to try new tactics as things are no longer working. I happily have a system that is working very effectively for me at the moment, which includes color-coding my calendar and blocking out specific time for tasks, and my ever-present to-do list.

Ah, is there anything so satisfying as checking things off a list?

Other challenges I am learning to deal with and overcome are the general obstacles that come with working from home, dealing with my Generalized Anxiety Disorder and working against my unfortunate tendency to become a hermit, despite being a social person and an extrovert!

Even though I'm working from home, time management is extremely important to me and my success, just like it was when I was an 8:30

to 5:30 corporate salesperson. I think the unifying thing across all jobs and all industries is being able to effectively manage your time and to actually accomplish all of your priorities and tasks.

When you work from home or are an entrepreneur in general, time management and work-life balance is even more important, and may be the single most impactful thing in my business.

It's hard to turn off being an entrepreneur, and I have long tended to be available days, nights, weekends, anytime. I answered emails, I jumped on calls, I said yes to all "hey, can you edit this super quick?" questions which came my way. I had to learn to turn it off, disconnect, and spend time with my family or a good book. This happens to be an ongoing learning experience.

I don't need to be constantly available. I am providing a service and high value to my clients; I am finally figuring out I don't need to sacrifice all my time to my work and my clients. Yes, my clients' needs are incredibly important to me. But so is my health and happiness and my family and home life. Finding that balance has been a difficult but necessary road.

Since I am trying not to be available at 10:30 pm on Saturday night anymore, I need to be as productive as possible during my business hours and manage my time wisely, in order to get everything done!

Managing time effectively does not mean just staying busy for the day, it means being productive and finishing the tasks and projects that need to be done, not just clicking around and checking email!

Here are some tips for time management which can really help you have a productive day, and allows you to get offline and enjoy life after work!

1. Daily/Weekly To-Do Lists
This is something that has helped me immensely! I tried to get into bullet journaling, but I am not a Pinterest-worthy bullet journaler and it didn't stick. The thing that has stuck is the daily listing of to-dos. Every morning, I read over my list of all the things I want to

accomplish that week and I add in or star things which need to be done that day.

I don't know about you, but checking things of a list is super satisfying for me! I move to-dos up from the week before if needed, and deadlines are written next to the task if there are specific due dates.

By rewriting the list weekly and adding to it daily, I am cementing my tasks in my head and able to really prioritize what needs to be done first.

2. Schedule in Some Down Time
At the office, people get lunch breaks, smoke breaks, walk around breaks, etc. You can't expect yourself to focus for 8 hours nonstop every day; it just doesn't happen and isn't realistic. Instead of giving yourself unrealistic expectations and then being disappointed when you don't meet them, make sure to give yourself some down time.

I start every day with coffee and checking Facebook. I check my email and my social media marketing as well. But I START with coffee, petting my cat, and reading Facebook before jumping into work.

Next, I read over my to-do list, check off anything I finished and add anything I need to, and make note of what I need to finish that day, and get started. At lunch time, I generally log off the computer and eat while I read a book or have a one-sided conversation with my cat. In the afternoon, I might go take a walk, or go to the gym, or just get up and stretch.

Have priorities and tasks for each day, but allow yourself to walk around, read the news, and text your friends, too.

3. When Working, Block Out Distractions
Like with down time, schedule specific work time. Use a calendar or an alert or whatever gets you ready to work, to let you know it's time to do this task or that activity or call that person.

When it's time to get down to business, do the task. Close out your social media tabs, and focus on the specific activity you need to complete.

In my case, I have several clients I do weekly blogging for. That means on Mondays and Tuesdays, I have to block out time to work on specific client blogs. I will do something like "10 am: Research and write blog for X client on topic Y."

When that time comes around, I turn off Facebook, put my phone face down, research and write the blog, edit it, and turn it into the client for review. If it takes an hour, great. If it takes two hours, awesome. As long as it gets done.

It all gets done faster when I'm not allowing my mind to wander to Instagram or texting my husband pictures of our cat.

And when work gets done faster, I feel better about it than when it takes hours or days because I just can't focus on it. My clients are happy, I'm happy, it's rad.

4. Stay Organized

This fits right into my to-do lists. Staying organized saves me time and energy, and most importantly, keeps my client information and needs at the forefront. As a solo practitioner, if I lose track of a client or forget to do something for them, I risk losing a major source of my income!

Remember: it is a lot less expensive to keep a current client than it is to find and attract new ones.

Keeping contracts, invoices, tasks, priorities, client needs, and my work organized is one of the largest parts of my success.

I use my calendar to track my client calls, my physical to-do lists for daily tasks and priorities, Google Drive for all of my documents and spreadsheets, and a physical filing cabinet for copies of my contracts and business receipts.

Find what works for you, and don't be afraid to say that something is NOT working, and try something different. Ask friends what they do to stay organized. I tried several things that didn't work before figuring out that scheduling everything in my calendar and getting reminders 30 minutes ahead of time really kept me on track. I tried physical calendars, post it notes of important tasks, and other things. It's about finding what works for you without annoying you.

Much like an alarm clock at 5 am, if it's annoying, you won't like it and will try to ignore it. Find what works for you, and try several versions to see what works best. Being adaptable and flexible is imperative when you are testing out new systems. Be willing to admit "Hey, this is not getting done; I need to try something else this time." It's totally okay to be wrong, but it's not okay to just keep doing it that way because you're used to it, even though it doesn't work.

5. Learn to Say No
This has been one of the hardest things for me to learn and is something I still struggle with and work on. I want to be indispensable to my clients, and also prove my value over and over, so I tend to say yes to anything they ask of me. I'm also somewhat of a people-pleaser in general.

This will lead me to being overwhelmed with work if I didn't really have the time for whatever I said yes to doing. I could miss deadlines or be overworked, or be working until late at night, like I did when I was working two jobs. I still sometimes find myself overbooked and working on client stuff at 10 pm on Tuesday evening. This is a work in progress!

I love writing and editing and being an entrepreneur, but I can't be everything to everyone. I am still working on saying no when I don't have time for something or if it is not part of the scope of my work or what I'm paid to do.

ProTip: Don't Ever Work for Free
Especially say no to doing work for free! Even a trial article for a new client is paid work, though often at a discounted rate. Do not give away your work for free. You are a professional, and your time and skills are valuable. Obviously, an exception to this rule is when you are purposely doing something as a volunteer.

In the end, I have to protect my time and keep my work from completely overrunning my home life. In order to be a good wife, daughter, friend, and individual, these time management skills have been extremely important in my personal and professional evolution.

I work from home, which is completely new for me. I've been in an office for the last 10 years. Before that I worked as a waitress in high school and college, and previous to being in restaurants, I was at a desk in school every day.

I am loving this life and my new career, and this is the first time in my adult life I am genuinely excited to go to work every day and the first time I've made my own schedule.

The positives far outweigh the negatives in my new lifestyle. I can travel more (and have!), as I can work from anywhere with wifi (like a New Orleans cafe, or my brother's house). I can make my own hours (all of them), I can stay in my PJs and not shower that day (it happens). I can take on new clients or not. I get to choose the type of work I'm doing. I am my own boss.

But there are certainly a few small drawbacks. It's easy to oversleep. It's easier to slack off when no one is watching. It's easy to keep working well past business hours. It's easy to get distracted. It's easy to eat poorly or snack too often.

I thought I was going to finally have time to go to the gym again. When I was working full-time and also building this business, I was working every evening until bedtime and all weekend long. It was a constant grind, and I loved it, but I was busy every waking moment. Previously, I'd gone to the gym 3-4 days every week!

Now, I am finding it all too easy to snack all day, much more than ever before, and then get caught up and busy and suddenly, the husband is home from work, I wrap up my day, and then I want to hang out with him, not leave and go to the gym. When I have time between calls during the day, I'm not going to the gym, I'm writing, organizing, working, marketing, etc. I don't have an hour and a half chunk of time to run errands and go to the gym, it's more like 20 minutes here or half an hour for lunch.

I've gained about 10 pounds, which I'm feeling badly and insecure about. But again, I love what I'm doing and that is my own fault for not having self-control! So, while I am a little stressed out about gaining a few pounds, it doesn't detract from my confidence in my writing and my work.

Working from home means I'm spending more time with my cat, less time with people, and have found it all too easy to stay home for several days at a time. It can be an issue, because I don't have a ton of friends in NY, and I am getting isolated. It can be very isolating to be the only person you know in your city who works from home. I find it all too easy to get busy, stay busy, and stay home.

To address this, my plan is to try to get out of the house and:

- Take walks.
- Go with my neighbor and her kids to the park once a week.
- Find somewhere to volunteer in the neighborhood.
- Try to get back to the gym.
- Take half-days on Fridays and go into the city.

One Friday, I took the afternoon off and went into the city to meet up with my old boss and some friends for lunch and then drinks, and it was great! I felt like my old self, but better. So, I am trying to make every Friday a half-day (or more realistically, a three-quarter day) and either go meet up with people in the city or go to the gym and enjoy some time to myself.

My biggest challenges in working from home and for myself have been time management and a bit of loneliness, and trying not to become a hermit. Sometimes I find myself so busy and productive I don't leave the house at all! When that happens, my husband comes home from work wanting to relax and I have just saved up all my words for him and need to give them all to him immediately.

I am constantly trying to improve. I want to learn, grow, build, make money, write more, and do better every day. So, when I am able to identify what I'm doing wrong, I can work on myself and do better next time!

Being an entrepreneur is great and I am truly happier than ever, but it can also be stressful, isolating, and a bit lonely, and I need to make sure my physical and mental health are properly addressed, not just my business. I used to love going to the gym because it was my "me time," and now I am having "me time" all the time! Maybe that has been a stumbling block as well.

I guess the advice I am trying to give myself is this: it's a lot of change, you're still figuring it out, 10 pounds isn't that big of a deal, you're working on it. Relax! You're doing great!

Anxiety is an insidious, sneaky, mischievous disorder which is hard to see. Much like insomnia or depression, it feels somewhat relatable, so many people don't think it's that big of a deal.

"Oh, you have anxiety? Yeah, I was super stressed last week, I totally get it."

"Oh, you have depression? I was sad when my friend moved away."

It is condescending to relate my diagnosed disorder which causes me daily suffering and uses most of my brain power to dwell on to that one time you couldn't sleep, were sad, or felt a bit anxious. I know you don't mean to, but when you try to compare your one-time difficulty to a person with anxiety or depression, it comes across as trivializing it.

You can't see anxiety. It isn't a physical scar, a broken bone, or a pros-thetic leg, and when we can't see something, we try to understand it in the context of our own experiences. That's human nature, and very understandable, but I would prefer you to ask questions or at least pretend, before assuming that someone's sometimes-almost-debili-tating disorder is 'no biggie.'

I was diagnosed with Generalized Anxiety Disorder when I was 19, and had diagnosed (and sometimes medicated) insomnia for several years prior to that. I did not take anti-anxiety medication. For a long time, I was using counting, breathing, and some meditation tech-niques to help me control it. The anxiety fed into the insomnia, and I would get stuck on a loop in my head, unable to sleep.

It got worse over the years, and I counted more, breathed more, slept less. I would sometimes go through "bad" cycles of insomnia where I was only sleeping an hour or two every night. It would last about two weeks, and I sometimes would get physically sick from my weakened immune system. I'd take an Ambien to try to reset my sleep cycles. Sometimes it worked, sometimes it didn't.

I always tried not to let anxiety keep me from the things I wanted to do and enjoy doing, like skydiving, riding huge scary roller coasters, traveling internationally, swimming with stingrays, driving ATVs through a jungle in Mexico, and more. Life is more fun when you do things that scare you.

I did all of those things. But I always had to squash or ignore the anxiety to do it.

By 30, the anxiety had grown to the point where every single day I was anxious about multiple "what would I do if the bridge collaps-es/a gunman appears/a bomb explodes?" **My life was made up of worst case scenarios**. I would get very anxious inside, a knot in my stomach, heart beating faster, brain going a mile a minute, until I mentally decided how I would react to any given situation, before I could start to relax. I kept it inside, trying not to show any signs of my anxiousness to others, which led to unintentionally hiding it.

This was my normal. Every bit of turbulence on a flight convinced me of my impending death, walking up a long flight of stairs made me question what would happen if I slipped and fell down them, and I was constantly trying to calculate how far from a bridge/train platform/plane I could fall and still live.

Hours per day of worst case scenarios, and I didn't even realize how much I was really effected. It happened over time, from being a little anxious and thinking some about different possibilities, before gradually growing in my mind to these horrific events I had to figure out how I would react to. I was still working and productive, but this would constantly be hovering in the back of my mind.

It grew so slowly, and I have always tried to be very aware of my emotions so that if I were feeling erratic or anxious, I could monitor myself and try to talk myself off the ledge.

And then I started my own business. I was working full time in my day job and building my business on the side. I was working 70-80-hour weeks, including weekends.

It was stressful, and I was surprisingly not super anxious about it.

Being a writer and editor relies on my skills, specifically on skills I am extremely confident in, and I have always been a hard worker. I was working every night from the moment I got home from the office until bedtime, as well as over the weekends, to get writing assignments done and take client calls.

The writing didn't make me anxious, but the idea of leaving a perfectly good job and career and steady paycheck, of course there was some anxiety there. But for some reason, having multiple clients relying on me and being so extremely busy all the time was not triggering overwhelming anxiety.

There was a bit of a cloud over my head when I thought about working from home full time, but mostly I was excited. It's funny. Little everyday things caused unending anxiety and tightly-clenched stomach muscles, balled fists, and the occasional migraine, but this huge, life-altering decision felt easy and right.

Even though I wasn't specifically anxious about entrepreneurship, my heavy, daily anxiety about everything and anything continued to weigh on me. In a big admission, I finally decided to ask for help. I'm incredibly lucky that my husband supports my choices, tries to understand my anxiety, and has often taken a primary role in talking me down with what seems to be a combination of hugs and distractions

For a long time, I tried to stay quiet about my anxiety with him. It wasn't his problem, and I didn't want him to think I was crazy. I finally started letting it out, and while he probably thinks I'm a bit nuts, he truly tries to understand what I go through and how I feel. He holds my hand when we fly and always takes the upper level when we drive on the Verrazano Bridge, knowing that I have thought much too long and too hard about this bridge. I want to drive on the upper level because if anything were to happen, the lower level could catch us (I realize how ridiculous that is).

When I need to unpack and really talk through my emotions and how I'm feeling, he allows me to just talk and he listens. He asks questions, discusses my reactions, and doesn't try to minimize it. He just lets me feel. I have trained myself to keep a careful watch over how I'm feeling so I can always catch myself if I am overreacting or feeling erratic and try to figure out why.

I spoke to my doctor and in late 2016 I started my first ever low-dose anti-anxiety medication. Honestly, even the thought of taking the meds made me anxious and kept me up at night. They said it would take about 4 weeks to fully kick in, and I spent the first 2 weeks battling a light dizziness that lasted all day. I almost quit, because I didn't think it was working. If anything, it was distracting me from working at the level I needed to be, especially given how busy I was.

Week 3, I felt a difference. The dizziness faded, and almost without me noticing, I started to mentally gnaw on things much less. About a week later, I had a sudden realization that I hadn't once thought about dying that day. Sounds simple, maybe, but I haven't gone a day without thinking about potentially deadly scenarios for as long as I can remember.

It's been a significant weight off my shoulders, my chest, and my sleeping habits. I'm sleeping better than ever, I am more focused and less distracted, and I am finally able to live without constantly thinking about dying. It's not erased, the anxiety still exists, but it's muffled now, and I can live my life without constantly dwelling on it. I still have sleeping issues, but they aren't as bad or as constant as before, and I have to take an Ambien significantly less often.

I'm a business owner, with everything that entails. Marketing myself, new client prospecting, proposals, writing, editing, project and time management, being at home with my cat, managing myself, and more. I love it. There will always be some anxiety, but I know deep inside myself this is what I should be doing. **And I refuse to let anxiety rule my life or keep me from my dreams.**

I also refuse to keep my anxiety hidden. **This is a part of who I am and I absolutely refuse to be a part of stigmatizing mental health in this country.** We are doing our citizens a huge disservice by not taking mental health more seriously, whether it is for veterans, children, or anyone else. We don't talk about it in a positive light, and I for one am proud of taking a step toward controlling it.

I don't want to be on medication forever as I don't enjoy having to rely on it, and am also taking steps to learn more meditation and other ways of personal development which have been shown to help ease the symptoms of anxiety, as well as other mental health issues, like depression. But for now, my medication is helping me. I am able to go a whole day without being anxious about death, which has never happened before. I know that sounds super morbid, but it really has just always been there. Until recently, I didn't know what it was like to not think about different worst-case scenarios all the time.

Though I'm not now, I've seen a therapist before, and found it to be beneficial.

Take care of yourself. Be healthy and happy. You are allowed to take steps to be mentally healthy and to talk about it, share your experiences, and answer questions about it. Don't let our society keep you from being open and honest about mental health issues, or make you feel like you're crazy for having one.

Our human brains are so complex, so intricate, and scientists don't know everything about them yet. Your depression or anxiety or PTSD, it's not something you can heal just because you want to. There are medications which can help correct the chemical imbalance in your brain. Would you blame your friend for having a heart defect? No, of course not. Then why would you blame yourself for a tiny brain defect?

You and me? **We are not broken, and I will not spend one second of my life believing that we are.**

Chapter 11:
Some Lessons Learned

I found out there is a whole new set of rules when it comes to being your own boss. I learned some lessons along the way and have definitely figured out most of them through basic trial and error. I'm still learning new lessons all the time. Here are some of the most important ones I had to learn: the perils of being too connected, breaking up with clients, and trying not to take criticism personally.

As an entrepreneur, you are basically always connected. Especially when you work from home, you're always at the office! It's easy to lose track of time and work too late, or "just answer this email super quick" at 10 pm or on a Saturday.

It's also your passion, so you want to keep working, keep delivering, keep proving yourself over and over.

You are valuable. You are worth the money. People are paying you because they believe you have the skills to do the work and deliver on your promises. You've already sold yourself, now you're just continuing the work of making yourself irreplaceable.

I get it. I honestly do. Hell, I'm writing this at 10:30 at night on a Monday, sitting on my couch and listening to "The Great British Baking Show" on Netflix in the background.

But the thing is, you and I…we deserve a vacation sometimes. We deserve to have dinner with our families without a phone in one hand. We deserve time off now and then.

When I was working in corporate sales, it was easy to leave work at the office and turn my mind to other things at home. I might've given my email a cursory glance over the weekend, but I didn't feel like I had to be glued to my computer. I took my earned vacation days and I went away for a week, while only checking email and checking in with the office once or twice.

Now, I just spent 5 days in Florida, in gorgeous weather with family, amazing food, a beautiful wedding, and perfect beaches. Every day, I was still checking email and responding, I got work done while I was there, and even spoke to some clients!

Why did I feel like I owed my clients my time off, in addition to the work I do, the meetings, the time, effort, and energy spent during the week?

For the same reason I felt guilty when giving my resignation at previous jobs. I did all of the work, and often more, than I was paid to do. I was on time, a hard worker, and a friendly colleague. I helped people as much as I could. When I got an offer from a new company, I accepted it, and then immediately got a huge knot in my stomach. I had to go in and give my notice to my boss and I was dreading it. I still did it and was completely professional, but it was scary and nerve-wracking, and made me feel terribly guilty for leaving.

There was no real reason for guilt. I did the work I was paid to do and I was looking out for what was best for myself and my career, as you're supposed to do. My boss wasn't looking out for my career, the company owners weren't, that's my job and only mine.

That's how it is with your own business, too. You're doing the work you're being paid to do, and likely more. So why do we feel like we can't take the weekend off or go on vacation?

It's a process. I am trying to let go and take time for myself, and remember I do great work, and that's why I have awesome clients who stick with me.

We all deserve time off now and again, and we need to stop feeling guilty for wanting it. It's a learning process, realizing you don't need to respond immediately if someone emails you on a Saturday night, and figuring out they probably don't even expect it! I am slowly learning to let go, and trying not think about work in my off hours.

It's so easy to make work my whole life. It can be hard to disconnect and be a wife, a friend, a sister, a daughter. I actually scheduled my mother into my calendar this week, so we could have a nice talk!

As much as I love my work and my life, which is really a lot and I have never been happier, I can feel it becoming more stressful.

I have to step back, we all do. I have to remember I am allowed to have a life outside of work. Clients CAN wait a bit for me to respond to their emails, even until the next business day, if needed.

I'm allowed to go run errands, or go shopping, or even knock off a bit early if I want. I can make time for the gym.

I have to continue to remind myself of all of this, because it is so easy to fall into being so busy I have no time for myself.

I know it is important to have time to yourself. Time away from work, relaxing or doing something you enjoy which has nothing to do with calls, clients, and deadlines.

It is better for your brain and your overall health and well-being to step away and have time for YOU. If you aren't happy, mentally, emotionally, physically, then how can you give it your all in business and for others? If you can't care for yourself, how can you care for anyone else?

I officially, wholeheartedly, unequivocally give you permission to take time just for you.

No kids, no spouse, no questions. Whether that is the gym, taking a walk, having a drink, reading a book, going bowling, whatever makes you happy and lets you completely turn off work. I truly know how hard this can be, but it's so important.

Be healthy and be happy in all aspects of your life, and your work can only benefit!

One of the biggest perks of owning your own business is being able to say "no" to doing certain kinds of work or to clients you don't want to work with.

But what happens when you've already been working for a client for a while, and over time the scope of the project changes, to the point where you find yourself working on and doing things you didn't want to be doing?

It's normal to feel guilty for dumping a client. They have been paying you, you've been working with them for a while, maybe they are a really nice person, or you really like their company and what they're doing.

That's all fine. You can like a person and their product without wanting to work for them. I like Build-A-Bear and bought one for my niece, but I don't want to work there. I like pizza, but I don't want to work throwing dough.

I recently found myself in a situation where I had been doing writing and editing and documentation for a client, but over time it really turned more and more into sales and marketing research and working on business development, which was not what I wanted to be doing with the bulk of my time. I had to break up!

There are several things to consider when breaking up with a client, in the same way that you would have things to think about when quitting a job in the corporate world.

- Are you making enough money from your other clients that you can stop working with this one?
- If not, do you have another client lined up?
- Do you want to keep the door open to possibly work with the client again in the future?
- Are you in the middle of a project?
- Do you want to give them notice, giving them time to replace you?
- Are they paid up through now?

It's not wrong to want to stop working with people. You have your own business specifically so you can do the work you love. It would be one thing if it was the difference between eating that week and working with that person.

But you wouldn't be asking the question if that were the case.

It is OKAY to break up with a client.

There, I said it. Now here are some tips and a script for how to do it.

Most importantly, stop feeling guilty. You have been doing the work you were paid for, you've been responsive, helpful, useful, and easy to work with (assuming you are those things!).

Here are specific points to hit:

- Ask your client in an email if they have a moment to talk. Breaking up is best done over the phone (I am assuming you are not physically working with this person; if so, do it in person). Basically, set up a time where you can talk **one on one with no distractions.**
- **You are the one setting the agenda for this call.** When you get on the phone, start with something good about working with them: "It has been great working with you these last few months, and I have really enjoyed getting to know you and your company and products. The work we've been doing has been very interesting and challenging."

- Then go into the meat of the call, discussing **why you are moving on.** "What I'm working on now is really not what I want to be doing, and I appreciate the work, but this is not right for me at the moment."
- Next, **talk about timing**: "I know this current project has another 4 days, and I am going to continue and finish it, both because I am already working on it, and because you have already paid."
- **Make sure to discuss any upcoming or missing payments.** "I am happy to stay through the end of the month if you'd like, as that is how we typically bill for these services. Do you want to stop and pay now at a prorated amount, or would you rather me keep working through the end of the month and pay the full price, as our contract states?"
- **Offer to train someone new or be flexible** with ending, if you want. "I can stay for another two weeks or so at my current rate if you want me to train my replacement, or I can end today, whichever works best for you."
- **End with a compliment:** "I have enjoyed working with you, and I hope we get to work together again in the future."

This is just one way to say each of these things, but these are the high notes you want to hit. Start and end with complimentary things (a compliment sandwich!), talk about the specific timing for ending the work, and make sure to discuss any money you are owed. The point is that you want to keep things professional, as well as be clear about your needs, and not burn any bridges.

While it's normal to feel a bit bad when breaking up with a client, remind yourself you have nothing to feel bad about. You did the work you were paid for, and they certainly won't look out for your best interests. Bosses and clients don't, that is your job.

This is your career, your job, your life. You have to learn to say no to working with people you don't want to work with, learn to break up with current clients, and figure out exactly what it is you do want and work toward that.

This is basically the same way you would approach quitting a corporate job, as well. Thanking them for the opportunity, putting in notice, and discussing details. Keep it professional and leave the door open to working together in the future.

I'm not saying it's easy, but I am saying it's important to know how to break up with a client, and how to say no to new prospective clients who are asking you to do work you don't want to do or are not an expert in.

Criticism. Just as in life, not everyone is going to like you, and not everyone is going to want to work with you.

Anything approaching art is subjective. Great ad writing is completely different but not *less* than great story writing. Oil paintings are different than watercolors, though they are both art. If my writing style isn't right for one client or job, it will be right for another. Besides, if I took every criticism personally, I would never be happy!

As a writer, I put a piece of myself in everything I write, but this is especially true for major projects like ghostwriting a book. When a blogging client asks me to make changes or says they don't like a certain part of the post, I feel nothing. I don't feel insecure about my writing, or bad that they don't like part of it; I just simply make the requested changes.

But when I've spent 2 months and dozens of hours with a client and their story and putting it together into an entire book, I can't help but get defensive when it's criticized. I don't mean to, and I feel bad for immediately getting defensive, and I always apologize.

But I can't help it. I poured a bigger piece of my heart and soul into that book, and when it's a creative criticism or something completely ambiguous, I get nervous and defensive and probably a bit argumentative. Especially when it's a subjective criticism like "I want it to have more WHABAM!"

I don't know what that means, can you give me a specific example? "You're the writer. You know, more BOOYAH!"

And it's not malicious or mean or meant to be harsh from the client. They don't know how to describe what they mean and I don't understand what they need. It can be frustrating and has certainly led to tears (mine) when I thought a client wanted a project practically rewritten, and in the end, they just wanted a small piece to be described a little differently.

Writing is an art and the writer is bringing stories to life using their imaginations and a good thesaurus. I can certainly be temperamental about my art and I am continuing to grow and learn.

As a ghostwriter, it is simply something I must get over. I can still pour my heart into the book, but I have to keep reminding myself it isn't MY book, and that the original author is allowed to make changes and have ideas and like things done his own way.

This is a constant work in progress!

I think learning not to take criticism personally is an important part of growing within your career. In the corporate world, it is your boss's job to make sure you understand all pieces of your work, answer questions, and correct you when you make mistakes. They train you, teach you, evaluate you, and try to tell you ways you can improve. Learning to take that advice and criticism and work with it, improve my work, and not take it as a personal attack was a very important part of my career growth and in my relationships with my bosses.

Unfortunately, when it is a paying client or when you're trying to criticize yourself, it's a whole different ball game, and I am still learning how to adapt and grow in response to this type of learning opportunity. It's so different than having a short meeting with your boss and both spit balling ideas of how to improve certain processes, or a trainer saying, "No, do it this way. It is better because…"

I am learning on the fly for this, as critiques of my writing is a fairly new experience for me. All of my blogs and articles online are basically accepted as they are, as a singular piece of finished work. I wrote them, they are published, and people usually accept them as finished pieces and when they comment, it's about the content.

But when you're ghostwriting a book, it is not a finished piece and it isn't even my story to tell. That is the difference. I am telling someone else's story, and his heart and soul is in every word as much as, if not more, than mine is. I have to remind myself that this story is his. He lived it and learned from it, grew from it, and came out the other side. It's not my story, I am just helping get the words out. That is what helps me when the work is criticized, or the client had questions or concerns. This is his life, and the accuracy and the way it ends up is more important to him than my argument for a specific turn of phrase or wording.

Chapter 12:
Learning Curves & What's Next?

I am focused on figuring out and implementing my long-term goals. As I have been in business and seen what works and what doesn't for me, and been exposed to so many different types of writing, I've been able to really form new goals and pathways. Exciting ones! I am currently under contract to write a comic book, something I never would have thought of doing! I'm ghostwriting books, a path I had never once considered, and one it turns out I love.

I have a brand-new offering which I love, book coaching. I am working with authors one-on-one to help them put together an outline and write their book. I do accountability check-ins, brainstorm with them, discuss challenges and obstacles, celebrate triumphs, edit their work, and assist them in the publishing process. I had never even heard of book coaching before becoming a writer for hire, and it has turned into an immensely satisfying and constantly surprising new path in my career.

I'm also still really learning my limits. I have lessened the total number of clients I have, and am trying to protect my time better. It's so easy to be working all the time, or to want to take on just one more client because the project sounds so interesting!

Learning to stop working is difficult when you're working for yourself and doing something you enjoy! But time is a commodity and you cannot work every moment. I have fewer clients now, but they pay more than my first ones did, and they find my services valuable and necessary.

I hope I am not giving the impression that starting my own business has been all sunshine, rainbows, and oatmeal cookies.

It hasn't.

I was suspended from contributing to *Huffington Post* after accidentally violating their terms of service, which was a huge blow. I let clients talk me down to a price I wasn't comfortable with because I wasn't pushing back and showing/understanding my value well enough. I let a client be almost 60 days late paying me because I knew they were going through something personally. I found typos and grammatical errors in a book I edited and paid out of pocket to have the book fixed and republished from my own mistakes.

Each of those has been a learning experience. Each of those has taught me something new to watch out for. Each one of them and all of my other mistakes and failures have been learning opportunities.

We try to have "teachable moments" with children whenever something goes wrong. We give them an allowance in exchange for chores to try to teach them the value of money. We break up sibling fights and tell them about peaceful conflict resolution. After consoling the kid who was teased, we try to explain that not everyone is going to like you and you have to ignore the haters. We allow them to choose their own haircuts and pick out their own clothes so they learn body autonomy.

But what about as adults? Especially business owners? No one sits you down and talks about how that missed deadline and the loss of a client is really going to drive home the importance of organization, prioritization, time management, and meeting deadlines.

No one tells you how creating the wrong pricing structure is going to eventually benefit you by showing you what doesn't work or how undervaluing yourself is a lesson about the value of your time.

Unfortunately for entrepreneurs, as much as you may try to learn, research, write, think, talk, and dream, sometimes you will fail.

You'll fail a little teeny tiny bit, like when you flub a pitch and lose out on a new client.

You'll fail a medium amount, when you underprice yourself and didn't realize how long something would take, and you eat ramen for a couple of nights.

You'll fail big.

It happens. It really does. That's a cliché because it's true!

It's not about failing, because we all fail. No one is perfect and everyone has missteps, mistakes, failures, stumbles, whatever you want to call them.

Treat every failure as a learning opportunity. They're the best way to learn, really. Is there any better way to beat a concept into your head than to have real life stakes and emotions invested in it?

Failing at something does not define you.

How you react to failure does.

Do you pick yourself up and dust off and learn from it? Or do you cross your arms and pout and tell anyone who will listen how it's not your fault?

Do you attack the problem from a new angle? Or do you insist everyone else was wrong and you were right and can't comprehend or accept why it didn't work?

Are you the type of person who will really look at the problem and figure out why it didn't work, so that you can succeed next time? Or the type to give up and quit since 'it didn't work anyway'?

What type of entrepreneur are you and what type do you want to be?

We all fail. Big, medium, or small, failures are part of business and life. Failures cannot define you or your ultimate success. How you react to your own failures and proceed forward will determine your success in life.

When you first start a business, you really will just say yes and take any and all clients who come your way.

I was trying to price myself at the top of the bell curve for average per-word pricing, but mostly I was making it up as I went along, often undervaluing myself.

One of my early clients actually asked if I was interested in possibly setting up a monthly fee, and continuing to work together.

I confidently answered, "Of course. Let me send you a proposal."

As soon as I hung up the phone, I started to do some math.

"OK, if I am doing 4 blogs per month, and each blog takes me 3 hours to come up with a topic, research, write, edit, revise, and post, then that is 12 hours per month. If I charge $300, then that is $25 per hour. Respectable, but I am currently making a lot more than that per hour. Well, they also mentioned possibly needing editing for website copy, so I should build in some padding. OK, $400 feels good."

And that's how I got to $400 per month for my first monthly retainer. In the end, I was still underestimating and undervaluing my time, but it was a great learning experience.

I also researched different contracts online, finding and tailoring the wording to suit my needs and to have very clear descriptions. I even had a lawyer friend look it over! I was all set. My contract lays out very specific hourly expectations, deliverables, even intellectual property ownership.

As soon as I started working with a couple of monthly clients, I was able to see that was the direction I needed to go. I loved having regular, specific work, building relationships with my clients, the steady pay, and the stability.

As I continued to build my business, I got referrals, continued to market myself, and networked. I soon got up to nine monthly clients!

I was busy, I had steady, reliable income, and could work on long-term projects. It was far more gratifying than writing a single blog post or article.

Over time I have whittled that down to five monthly clients, and am actually making MORE money with five than I was with nine, because I have been able to scale up my pricing and also take on more work with the clients I have, versus finding additional ones.

I still like to have a project, such as ghostwriting or editing a book, outside of my monthly clients, because I love doing those things. Those bigger projects make me happy, and I love being exposed to new books and being involved with them, in addition to my daily work.

My clients are a combination of weekly blogging, ghostwriting, editing, and other projects. I have so much variety, and I love every moment of it.

The beauty of having a monthly subscription business model is you have a reliable income coming in, but with such diversity in the work I'm doing, I get to stay on my toes and stay interested in what I'm doing and with whom I'm working.

Now, when a prospective client comes to me and asks about pricing and working together, I tell them about my monthly fees, what that might include, and we discuss their specific needs. I no longer start with the per-word pricing; I launch directly into talking about how I structure my monthly clients, my time, our weekly calls, and what I can do for them.

I have been able to scale up my pricing. This came as a byproduct of learning how much time different things really take and my overall compensation goals.

I love that the monthly business model came to me from a client, and I have been able to continue using it and growing and expanding my business and my skills. I certainly make significantly more money than I did when I was taking on various singular articles, making peanuts!

I no longer market myself as doing one-off articles and blogs. In fact, I really don't market myself at all anymore. My monthly clients and I have built great relationships, and they refer people to me and recommend me to people all the time. Most of my current clients came from referrals!

Referrals are extremely important when you're an entrepreneur and the best possible compliment. People who are referred to you are coming from a trusted source and are already feeling good toward you and your work, based on the simple fact that you were recommended.

Every single person I speak to, whether they end up becoming a client or not, I always ask for referrals.

"Hey, it was great speaking with you/working with you! Do you know anyone who may need writing and editing services? I'd love to talk to them. I'll follow up with you soon!"

Even if they didn't end up becoming a client of yours, they did talk to you and get a feel for who you are and the work that you do. It is free to ask for referrals and the return is typically huge. Not everyone will have someone to refer to you, but plenty will. Even if it is several months later!

Continuing to refine and streamline the business and being adaptable is a major part of entrepreneurship. I am refining my offerings, and learning to say "no" to work I'm not interested in doing.

I am starting to put together an email list, so I can send out relevant information or updates to people. This is something I really should have been doing from the start and I just didn't know why I should or how it would benefit me, or even how to create a subscriber list.

You should start collecting emails ASAP. People who follow you and want to read your writing will be interested in a monthly newsletter, or in an email when you publish your book. I really wish someone had told me that at the beginning.

I've loved meeting other writers. It is always a pleasure to meet others who are absolutely in love with their career. I still sometimes feel like a fraud, like I don't fully belong, but it is a growing process. Sometimes I feel like a kid playing dress up as a grown up, too, but I am so happy to have this life.

I am also meeting and learning from other entrepreneurs! I don't always have to do things the hard way, and can learn from other people's mistakes.

Just as I hope you do, from mine. My first few clients were only being charged $0.05 per word. That is just $50 for a 1000-word article. It ended up being less than $7 per hour! I learned very quickly that was not sustainable.

As I mentioned, I am focused on figuring out my long-term goals. My ultimate goal is to continue streamlining my services and scaling my prices up, so I can have 3-4 monthly clients total, making at least what I'm making now, plus one larger project. This way, I'll be able to focus on my relationships with each client, the work I do for them will grow and expand, and I'll be making more money overall.

I also have really enjoyed starting to work as a book coach, and find satisfaction in helping a writer go from concept to completing their book. It's so amazing! I want to be doing more of this and really seeing that build into a main pillar of my work.

The highest I got was 10 clients at the same time, and I am currently at seven. Five are monthly, two are projects, and I am above $5,000 per month, every month. I want to be even higher!

What is next for me?

For the rest of my career, I want all of my clients to be referrals. That is my dream. I want to be so good at what I do that clients want to stick with me, see my value every day, and recommend me to people.

How did I get all my referrals? I am completely happy to share my secret with you.

The secret is being extremely easy to work with and collaboration. Being good at building relationships, marketing yourself, and having strong skills are the backbone of any successful person or profitable business.

I keep my clients completely involved and knowledgeable about what I am doing at all times. A perfect example of this is how I approach editing a book.

Writing a book is like putting a piece of your soul on paper. As much as you know you need to have it edited, no one really wants to hand off their book, their baby, to a stranger and not see it or have any information for a month or more.

I've had authors come to me, nervous and upset, because their last editor completely restructured or changed major parts of their book. Not only were they horrified, but they also were made to feel like their book wasn't good enough. And that is a personal insult!

The author had no idea their book was being torn apart and sewn haphazardly back together, because they handed it off to some editor weeks before.

When I am editing a book, I want it to be an easy experience for both the author and me. Especially the author! I know how heart-wrenching it is to open yourself up to criticism and revisions. It's physically painful and quite stressful!

That's why I put their entire book into a Google doc, and give them commenting/suggesting permission. I go through the document making all grammar, punctuation, syntax and other grammatical changes, and then adding comments throughout with suggestions on word choice, structure, and asking questions if I don't understand something or see inconsistencies. Editing for content and flow is exhilarating and so much fun! I love when an author tells me that I pointed out something which contradicted something else in the plot. It's great for both of us that we caught it and fixed it.

The author can pop in and out of the document whenever he wants, answering comments, asking questions of his own, and even making suggestions, which I can respond to, accept, or reject.

We also have a weekly check in call to discuss progress and see how he is feeling about my edits and changes, and answer any questions he may have. The author is always up to date on progress, timing, and more. I am accessible and available, and he can always see what I'm doing to his book.

The authors I've worked with have found this to be extremely comforting, and know they can tell me, "No, I don't like that change" and I will change it back.

That's my secret. I work in a way which lets the author know what's going on, and it is a very collaborative edit. They won't need to go do more revisions, and when I'm finished, the book is ready to go to the formatters. I've had several authors tell me that I've been the best editor they had ever worked with simply because they felt so involved and up-to-date.

It's a matter of empathy. If this were MY book/blog/website what would I be most comfortable with?

Being a book editor and working for a publisher has long been a dream of mine, so to realize that dream and then actually be good at it is incredibly gratifying.

Basically, I am letting my business adapt and change as needed. I thought I would mostly be a blogger and that did not turn out to be true. Thankfully! I love these new avenues which I didn't even realize would be options for me. A big part of that is networking and meeting people who gave me new opportunities, and another huge part is I was open to new possibilities and always eager to try something different.

90 days. It took me three months from getting my first client to quitting my full-time job.

But that was just the beginning.

Conclusion:
This is Only the Beginning

The real secret of entrepreneurship is you never do it alone. Your free time will no longer exist and you'll work harder than you thought possible. You will be excited, exhausted, and exhilarated.

All of my relationships suffered from lack of time during this process. It was a relatively short time, but I was incredibly busy and unavailable for a while. I spoke to my best friend and my parents less than ever, I wasn't going out and doing anything; my husband was basically abandoned.

But I could not have done it without them. My husband is truly one of the most patient, supportive, amazing people I have ever met. From the very first day that I called him in the middle of a work day to tell him I got my first client, he has been excited, encouraging, and supportive. He could have been cautious or wary and I would have understood.

The first time I was published in *Lifehack* and later, *Huffington Post*, we celebrated. When he comes home from work, I tell him everything I am doing with clients and what I work on, and any challenges. He knows all about them.

In all honesty, I could never have done any of this, taken such a big risk, without a Geoff-sized safety net beneath me. His support and encouragement to fulfill my dream, and him being okay with the potential lack of income, the long nights, the work, me ignoring him, and how much I talk about it all is how I survived. The way he listens when I talk about new projects and comforts me when I get overwhelmed is why I like him.

I became an LLC, and we celebrated. I worked all evening, and he left me alone and ordered us food. I have hang-ups about money and worried so much about lowering our income, and he reassured me and made sure that we had goals in place, and we could do this together.

I laugh at him, because he's so proud of me, and I love it. Someone recently asked what I did for a living, and before I could answer, Geoff proudly proclaimed, "She quit her job!"

I jumped in to explain I'd recently quit a corporate job to be a writer. It perfectly explains us.

He is as proud of me for chasing my dream as I am of him for always continuing to work on his. As a Lead DevOps Engineer, some of his work goes over my head, but he always explains it to me so I can understand, and answers all my questions to better understand what he is working on. His passion for technology and his career is what genuinely inspired me and pushed me over the edge into chasing my own passion.

He was one of those people who I have always been jealous of. He knew from a young age what he wanted to do with his life, got a Computer Science degree and then started working in the technology field right away.

In school, I saw people around me working toward being chefs, doctors, computer specialists, geologists, veterinarians, teachers, and other professions, and I never quite understood where that certainty came from.

I have a Bachelor's in Anthropology, which was incredibly interesting to learn about and I loved it. But I did not want to stay in school long enough to get a doctorate and then do anthro field work, so I knew I wasn't going to be an anthropologist for a career. I had no idea what I would do for the rest of my life.

When I was a kid, I wanted to be a singer, an astronaut, and a writer. In that order. I didn't know how to accomplish any of those, and just enjoyed them all as hobbies. I sang in chorus in school and in competitions, and I wrote songs. I went to Space Camp, read astronomy books and learned about it in school. And I always kept a journal and wrote stories and poems.

But how do people figure out what they want to be when they are so young? My mom was a teacher for 37 years, something she always wanted. How do people just pick something and then figure out how to get there?

I don't know. I didn't understand how to take the things I loved doing and make them into a career. Sometimes I think about how unprepared I was for the real world. In high school and college, they don't teach you how to do your taxes, or how to apply for a mortgage, what questions you should ask and what to look for when you rent an apartment, how to properly apply to jobs and go through the interview process, or how to determine your career.

High school prepared me for taking standardized tests, and college prepared me for reading books, writing essays, and regurgitating facts. It sucks that no one taught us how to cook, or have a handyman class which teaches you simple plumbing, electrical, and handyman skills. When I graduated college, I didn't feel prepared for life or a career. I kind of had to figure it all out as I went.

In my 10 years in corporate America, I learned so much about businesses and how they run, how to make them more efficient, how to organize and prioritize things, customer service, sales, business relationships, networking, and so much more. Those years prepared me for being an entrepreneur in a myriad of ways. Being an ambitious young woman, I tried my best to learn as much as possible and grow within my career in each position I held, and was lucky enough to have exemplary management.

I was also incredibly fortunate and thankful to have the boss I did when I ended my sales career. Dan was my boss for almost half of my career, and he never stopped helping me learn and grow, encourage me to be a rockstar, praise my wins and figure out how to get over the losses. When I sat down and told him I wanted to be a writer, Dan hugged me and said good luck.

My family and friends have all been encouraging and excited. I acknowledge and appreciate the support system I have. Quitting my job to work for myself was less of a risk than it could have been because I had so many people rooting for me to succeed.

This book marks a huge step in my writing career. A book with my own name as the author. While it likely won't change my path right away, I am so proud of myself and pleased with the way it came together. My client and friend is publishing it, my mother is my editor, my husband gave me my first rave review, and my friends want to read it.

I am profitable. My business is sustainable. If nothing changes, then I will remain happy and excited.

Being a business owner has also taught me a lot about myself. I have discovered the depths of what I can handle, from pressure, to time commitments, clients, and stress. I have learned more about what I need to be happy and that I'm truly allowed to be happy and excited about my work. I've learned how to run a business and to make sure to think of it as a business and not just me in front of my laptop. I have learned the value of my skills and it is okay to fail sometimes, as long as I pick myself up, dust off the dirt, and keep moving forward.

I think this whole entrepreneurship journey has brought my husband and I closer together. We are both living our passions and happy with our careers, and now that I am working from home, we are thinking about the future of our family and our goals.

I know this journey is only beginning and I am really stoked to see what happens next.

I have never been happier, healthier, more passionate, and more in love than I am right at this moment.

And I will be able to say the same thing again tomorrow.

Will you?

What would make you passionate, fulfilled, and happy?

Author Bio

Jyssica Schwartz is a thirty-something with a husband, a cat, an apartment in Brooklyn, big dreams, and so very many words.

A full-time writer and editor, Jyssica is generally found posting pictures of food or cats on Instagram, pithy notes on Twitter, or discussing random thoughts on her Medium blog when she should be working.

Jyssica has a Bachelor's degree from the University of Florida, is a Gators fan, a Yankees fan, and unapologetically claims the Offspring as her favorite band.

You can check out her website at www.jyssicaschwartz.com and let her know how life is going and make sure to join her mailing list (Schwartz Freelancer News) to get occasional emails on writer-y stuff.

Printed in Great Britain
by Amazon